The Information

Society

The Information Society

AN INTRODUCTION
(Histoire de la Société de l'information)

Armand Mattelart

Translated by Susan G. Taponier
and James A. Cohen

SAGE Publications
London • Thousand Oaks • New Delhi

Histoire de la société de l'information

Translation © Sage Publications 2003
© 2001, Editions La Découverte & Syros, Paris, France

First published 2003

SAGE Publications Ltd
6 Bonhill Street
London EC2A 4PU

SAGE Publications Inc
2455 Teller Road
Thousand Oaks, California 91320

SAGE Publications India Pvt Ltd
32, M-Block Market
Greater Kailash – I
New Delhi 110 048

British Library Cataloguing in Publication data

A catalogue record for this book is available from the British
Library

ISBN 0 7619 4947 X
ISBN 0 7619 4948 8 (pbk)

Library of Congress Control Number: 2002114570

Typeset by Mayhew Typesetting, Rhayader, Powys
Printed and bound in Great Britain by TJ International,
Padstow, Cornwall

Contents

Acknowledgements

The publishers would like to thank the French Ministry of Culture for their translation grant.

Introduction

The conquest of the cyber-frontier is a sequel to the grand technological narrative of the conquest of space. The latter gave us the cliché 'global village', while the former has already enshrined the expression 'global information society'. The irresistible rise of the notions of 'information society' and 'information age' has become indissolubly linked to the spectacular rise in the use of 'global age' vocabulary. Alongside the two notions, a whole machinery of apologetic discourse has developed, including promotional sales pitches, official proclamations, trendy manifestos and scientific or quasi-scientific studies, purporting to show that these terms are self-evident. We are promised a new society that will necessarily demonstrate 'greater solidarity' and be 'more open and more democratic'. The referent of this inevitable 'Republic of Technology' has thus been sealed off from controversy and debate at the grassroots level. Yet the notion of a global information society itself is the result of a geopolitical construction. We tend to forget this under the heady effect of ongoing technological innovation. The aim of this book is precisely to unearth the foundations of this construction: in other words, its underlying assumptions.

A new ideology that dare not speak its name has become part and parcel of 'the nature of things' and suddenly ranks as the dominant paradigm of social change. The notion of the 'information society' carries with it a body of beliefs that release symbolic forces, which not only enable action, but in fact trigger it and orient it in certain directions rather than others. These forces set the agenda for action and research programmes run by governments and supranational policymakers. Witness the number of Ministries of Industry, Technology and Science throughout the world that have appended 'and the Information Society' to their names, or even abandoned their former label in favour of this new one.

The same beliefs guide the strategies for worldwide expansion devised by so-called 'global' companies. They have mapped out the way military and diplomatic institutions are to make war and peace. They have given rise to a definition of change and of 'novelty' focused exclusively on technological progress. They have universalised a new sort of 'common sense' to legitimise these choices and distinctions, as if they alone were possible or reasonable, when in fact they belong to a particular system of truth. This form of hocus-pocus is recurrent in contemporary history. Indeed, the scheme of the information society arose during the Cold War as an alternative to the two conflicting systems embodied by the superpowers, at the same time as the 'end of ideology' thesis.

The notion of the information society took formal shape in the wake of the invention of artificial intelligence machines during the Second World War. It became a standard reference in academic, political and economic circles from the 1960s. The manufacture of a world of images related to the 'information age' continued apace throughout the following decade. The true geopolitical meaning of the neologisms created at the time to designate the new society would not come to light until the eve of the third millennium, with the proclamation of what is usually called the 'information revolution' and the arrival of the Internet as the new public-access network.

The second half of the twentieth century has indeed witnessed the creation of belief in the miraculous power of information technology, but this should not obscure the long view of its development. As evidence, we might point to the early utopian yearning for a universal language, long before computer language gave concrete expression to it. As hope in the possibility of determining the classifying principles of a world language grew, the pursuit of the Holy Grail reappeared in the form of the 'Library of Babel', as large as the universe itself, encompassing all of human thought and storing all possible books – an important theme in the work of Jorge Luis Borges.

The stakes of the new digital universe are too multiform and interdisciplinary to be left to technological determinism alone. They concern a multiplicity of social, political and economic actors. This archaeology of the 'information age' is thus, at the same time, an invitation to rethink the complexities and contradictions involved in the way information and communication technologies are appropriated by each society, in a world-economy containing radical inequalities and conflicts of interest.

1 The Cult of Numbers

The idea of a society governed by information is inscribed, as it were, in the genetic code of the social project inspired by a blind belief in numbers. The idea arose long before the notion of 'information' appeared in modern language and culture. This social project, which took shape during the seventeenth and eighteenth centuries, enthroned mathematics as the model for reasoning and useful action. Thinking in terms of what is countable and measurable became the prototype for truthful discourse, and it determined the scope of their quest for the perfectibility of human society. The French Revolution marked a high point in the effort to give concrete form to the language of mathematical calculation, making it the yardstick for judging the quality of citizens and the values of universalism.

Organising thought

Algorithms

'If I were to choose a patron saint for cybernetics out of the history of science,' wrote Norbert Wiener, 'I would have to choose Leibniz. The philosophy of Leibniz (1646–1716) centres about two closely related concepts – that of universal symbolism and that of a calculus of reasoning.' The book from which this passage is taken laid the groundwork of this scientific discipline immediately after the Second World War (Wiener, 1948: 12). Indeed, the German philosopher-mathematician's thinking on the nature of logic marked an essential step in developing the idea that it is possible for thought to manifest itself in a machine. Leibniz came close to automating the thinking process by developing binary arithmetic and a *calculus ratiocinator* or 'arithmetic machine', which was a more efficient calculator than the one devised by Blaise Pascal. For Leibniz, the discovery of a 'starting point' in relation to which everything would fall into place was the guiding principle in his search for a 'new compass of knowledge'. His idea of compressing information with a view to economising on thought was also at work in the indexes and catalogues he envisaged as a tabular space with multiple entry points.

Leibniz's mathematics, which included subsets as well as relations, constituted the first theory of complexity and the first philosophical treatment of 'complication'; in other words, the multiplicity and variety of numbers and beings can be organised, classified and arranged into a hierarchy (Serres, 1968). Leibniz (and Newton, independently of him) developed differential calculus and integral calculus by reducing the fundamental operations of infinitesimal calculus to an algorithmic approach. Algorithms are orderly series of elementary operations taken from a finite repertory of operations that can be performed within a given time. They could not, however, be converted into the concept underlying automated data processing until they could be expressed in algorithmic writing. This was to be the contribution of the Irishman George Boole in 1854, who laid the foundations of the autonomous discipline of computer science that came into being a hundred years later.

For Leibniz and his contemporaries, more rapid methods of calculation were needed to meet the requirements of modern capitalism in its formative stages. With the expansion of overseas trade, a market emerged for the collection, storage, bureaucratic processing and dissemination of data intended for merchants, financiers and speculators. The growth of maritime navigation called for improved shipbuilding. The calculation of longitude became a key laboratory for developing a theory of production of regular motion and 'automatic machines to measure time' (pendulum clocks, watches, marine chronometers): the remote ancestors of computers. The new attitude towards time and space spread to workshops, trading counters, armies and public administrations.

Bacon's project for useful science

'The virtues of ciphers are three: that they be not laborious to write and read; that they be impossible to decipher; and, in some cases, that they be without suspicion' (Bacon, 1996: 232). This enigmatic observation dates from 1605 and is taken from the argument put forth by Francis Bacon (1561–1626), a philosopher and future chancellor of England, in favour of a science of facts. The theoretician of the experimental method was referring here to innovations achieved in 'the art of ciphering and deciphering'. His interest in cryptography dates from the period 1576–1579, when he was an adviser at the embassy in France. During this period of upheaval due to the wars of religion, Bacon developed a secret binary language for sending diplomatic messages. Each letter of the alphabet was converted into a simple combination of two symbols and each symbol corresponded to a different form of typography. The science of secret languages would prove to be a recurring factor in the history leading up to the development of intelligent machines in the twentieth century.

Francis Bacon never abandoned his obsession with secrets. His project for a 'Great Restoration', a far-reaching intellectual reform that would break away from the scholastic view of the world and from prejudices that could not stand up to experimentation, was combined with an imperative of national security (*securitas publica*). He held this view despite the fact that his manifesto in favour of the 'increase of science' opened with a call for constant, uninterrupted progress towards the aim of general understanding and universal harmony, and thus for efforts to achieve the happiness of all by 'liberating man from his condition'. In Bacon's writings, the word 'information' meant *intelligence* in the sense of information gathering. In a posthumous work entitled *New Atlantis* (1627), Bacon developed his plan to reorganise all knowledge in utopian fashion; the 'inquiry' designed to establish the 'cosmography' of the countries he visited could be assimilated to espionage. On the isle of Bensalem, no fewer than nine categories of scientists were at work, in accordance with a strictly hierarchical division of labour, collecting, classifying and processing information. In the organisation chart conceived to plan useful science, the members of only one of the categories, the twelve 'Merchants of Light', were allowed to leave the country and travel about the world in search of 'books, and abstracts and patterns of experiments'. They were told to 'gather Enlightenment wherever in the world it may grow' by gleaning everything concerning the sciences, the arts, techniques and inventions. Moreover, they could travel only if they hid their origins 'under the names of other nations (for our own we conceal)'. Access to the island was prohibited to foreigners or, at the very least, strictly regulated, in order to protect its inhabitants' knowledge and skills, which were far superior to those of the rest of the world. A testimony to this high level of scientific expertise was the acoustic laboratory, which had invented an *inanimatus nuncius*, that is, a 'means to convey sounds in trunks and pipes, in strange lines and distances'.

In 1662, Bacon's plan for the reorganisation of knowledge was given concrete form with the founding of the Royal Society of London for Improving Natural Knowledge by Experiments, at the initiative of the merchants of the City of London. To many, the House of Solomon, where the sages of the utopian island of Bensalem dwelled, foreshadowed this academy of the sciences. In 1666, France set up a Royal Academy of the Sciences, and an astronomical observatory a year later. The geodesists of the time were busy trying to determine whether or not the earth flattened out at the poles, which they linked to the search for an invariable, universal standard of length. A solution for calculating the arc of the earth's meridian, based on the metre, would have to wait until the French Revolution. In 1676, the Royal Observatory of Greenwich became the symbol of England's control of the seas.

A universal language

Leibniz's project for automating reason was only one facet of the search for an ecumenical language. It was in keeping with his philosophy, which bore the stamp of cosmopolitical humanism, and inscribed in his religious thought. Leibniz wanted to help bring people closer together, to unify not just Europe but 'the entire human species', because, he wrote, 'I consider Heaven to be the Fatherland and all people of good will to be fellow citizens of that Heaven.' In explaining the mechanism he had just invented for reducing numbers to their basic principles, such as the two digits of 0 and 1, he noted that a similar binary system had already been used in China four thousand years earlier, formulated by Fuxi, China's first philosopher, the creator of its monarchism and author of the *Book of Changes*, better known as the *I Ching* (Fuwei, 1996). He emphasised the similarity of form, transcending geographical boundaries, to justify his theory that only a language of signs could resolve the imperfections of natural languages, which are sources of discord and pitfalls for communication. He also dreamed of arousing the interest of the Chinese in the *Respublica Christiana*.

Francis Bacon thought there could be no restoration of the sciences without a critique of the 'idols of the public realm', the false ideas − religious or otherwise − conveyed by words or common language. The desire to be free from these *idola* was an incentive to search for a universal language. The dream arose of an 'a priori' philosophical language, able to function as an 'alphabet of human thought', or a language capable of organising and encompassing all knowledge. After all, hadn't Descartes himself come up with the idea of a new language in 1629, which he developed using a decimal numbering system? The increase in trade, along with the decline of Latin as the lingua franca, the downfall of which was definitively assured by the Treaties of Westphalia in 1648, also contributed to fuelling the search for a universal language.

The archetype of all universal language projects appeared in 1668 in *An Essay towards a Real Character and a Philosophical Language* by John Wilkins (1614–72). Wilkins, a clergyman who taught at Oxford and was the first secretary of the Royal Society, was spurred by reading an unknown (or apocryphal) Chinese encyclopaedist to construct an 'analytic language'. To do so, he divided the universe into forty categories or classes, which were then subdivided into sub-classes, which in turn were subdivided into species. He assigned a two-letter monosyllable to each class, a consonant to each sub-class, and a vowel to each species. For example, *de* meant 'element'; *deb*, the first element, fire; *deba*, a part of the element fire, or a flame.

Three centuries later, while tracking down 'arbitrary imaginings' or attempts to solve the chaos of knowledge by 'classifying the universe', Jorge Luis Borges unearthed and wrote about John Wilkins' project and his original model borrowed from the Chinese encyclopaedist. Borges' essay, published in a collection entitled *Inquisiciones*, was, in turn, to become the 'birthplace' of Michel Foucault's' work, *Les Mots et les choses* (Words and Things). Indeed, as he himself indicates, it was after reading the Argentine writer's commentaries that Foucault undertook his 'archaeological inquiry' into the historic moment, which he places in the transition from the eighteenth to the nineteenth century, when the *episteme* or configuration of knowledge characterising Western culture shifted as a result of the break between words and things. At that moment, a 'new positivity' came into being. 'Tabular' thought made it possible to 'set up an order' among beings and a 'division into classes'. The taxonomy proposed by this thinking led to 'words' and 'categories that lack all life and place'. The coherence between the theory of representation and the theory of language dissolved and words ceased to merge with the world.

> Language as the spontaneous *tabula*, the primary grid of things, as an indispensable link between representation and things, is eclipsed in its turn; a profound historicity penetrates into the heart of things, isolates and defines them in their own coherence, imposes upon them the forms of order implied by the continuity of time; the analysis of exchange and money gives way to the study of production, that of the organism takes precedence over the search for taxonomic characteristics, and, above all, language loses its privileged position and becomes, in its turn, an historical form coherent with the density of its own past. (Foucault, 1993: xxv)

The project for achieving universal knowledge and rationality was a new way of thinking about both reason and words, fuelling the belief in perfectly transparent meaning.

Territorial organisation

Statistics: the science of the state and of trade

Probability theory, the foundations of which were laid down by Pascal and Huygens around 1660, became a new means of objectivising human society. It offered a method for choice in the event of uncertainty. Statistics and arithmetic or political anatomy opened up a new territory for practical science.

In Germany, the pioneers of statistics were confronted by the new reality created by the Treaties of Westphalia (1648). These treaties signalled the beginning of the concept of the modern nation-state and its corollary, stable borders, and confirmed the break-up of the empire into a multitude of microstates. From 1660, *Staatkunde*, or 'state knowledge', promoted the development of nomenclature and tried to meet the needs of state organisation. In keeping with this pragmatic tradition, the notion of 'statistics' was first defined by Gottfried Achenwall (1719–1772) as the 'state science' or *Staatswissenschaft*. It was aimed at 'illustrating the excellencies and deficiencies of a country and revealing the strengths and weaknesses of a State'. His method of 'multiple entry tables' (*Tabellen*) was similar to systematic cataloguing and provided an overview of the various states classified in a row, according to a set of comparable characteristics (Lazarsfeld, 1970). Beginning in 1725, the procedure for conducting a census of the population drew scientific legitimacy from the bureaucratic practices of Prussia under absolutism. For a long time, England resisted the idea of a general census in the name of individual rights, which explains the use of the first random samplings. The tools of statistical observation developed within the conceptual framework of political arithmetic. In 1662, John Graunt made a systematic analysis of the registers of baptisms, marriages and deaths in London parishes. It was one of the first studies presented to the Royal Society, which saw in it a 'new light for the world'. In 1693, the astronomer Edmund Halley published his mortality tables. A new social role was starting to take shape, that of the 'expert' offering a fully developed language for the use of governments; these were people trained in practical knowledge who came from a variety of professions (Desrosières, 1993). There seemed to be no limit to the possible fields of application. Statistical techniques not only contributed to the new relationship between the monarchical state and the various social classes engendered by the bourgeois revolution, but were inextricably linked to a new form of commercially oriented rationality. One of Halley's major aims in developing mortality tables was to provide actuarial techniques to assess life insurance schedules. From now on, calculation would allow people to protect themselves against the future.

Geostrategic transformation

France was undoubtedly the country in which mathematical reasoning was most widely used in the sciences aimed at the strategic control of the 'body of the earth'. Sébastien Le Prestre de Vauban (1633–1707), the famous fortifications engineer of Louis XIV, played a leading role. One of his biographers has written that this 'man of the soil' was a 'great mover of earth who knew the contours of France the way a sharecropper knows the slope of his fields' and that as he built its fortified towns, he was also building the fortress of the nation-state (Halévy, 1923). In an age when wars dragged on and on, the 'frontiers' where he built his 'great immobile machines' were, indeed, the front lines of combat. Historians of military strategy agree that Vauban was the prototype of the geometrical mind. The period during which he built fortresses coincided with the 'military revolution' between 1670 and 1680 led by the Marquis de Louvois, Secretary of War under Louis XIV. The main revolutionary changes within the army included systematically applying science to war (and its corollary: creating a corps of engineers); setting up a civilian administration of war with its own *ad hoc* ministry; ending the hiring of mercenaries and introducing professionalism and discipline in the ranks; stabilising the military population in barracks; drawing up a promotion grid stipulating the rules of advancement by seniority; and developing improved firearms and knives (that is, generalising the use of flintlocks and abandoning the pike in favour of the familiar bayonet with a sleeve or socket that held the blade at the side of the barrel) (Guerlac, 1986).

Vauban's thinking about territory and how to organise it was given full expression in his conception of a 'fortification system'. His overriding concerns, namely his determination to build a continuous border held together by a 'chain of forts', linked by canals or a network of canalised streams or rivers, his overall, in-depth vision of defence and his requirement that fortresses serve not only for defence but also as a base for offensive operations; all required a thorough knowledge of the terrain on which the fighting would take place. Fortified towns had to be situated in such a way as to control the routes on their own territory and facilitate access to enemy territory. Fortification projects were accompanied by statistical monographs describing the local population and living conditions, along with the activities and resources of the fortified city and the surrounding countryside. The actual construction of the fortified town called for 'relief maps' (historians of war simulations have identified the relief map as a precursor of war games played on maps drawn to scale of actual sites where battles might take place, which did not come into widespread military use until the eighteenth century). Relief maps reproduced on a scale of $1/600^{th}$ entire cities with their fortifications and surroundings, particularly routes and bridges, over a wide area, up to twenty times that of the town itself. The relief map was a genuine synthesis of information for defenders of a town, sometimes serving as a *model* and some-times as a *portrait*, since building fortifications and drawing maps went hand in hand (Parent, 1982). To connect the links of the chain, Vauban gave priority, wherever possible, to water routes rather than land routes.

Nothing escaped his quantitative method. Vauban is consid-ered, along with the Englishmen Robert Hooke and Edmund Halley, one of the pioneers of meteorology. He was the first to gauge the size of mine craters. He began the systematic measure-ment of the time required for cannon fire, as well as for the excavation of a fortified town, from which he derived prin-ciples for the organisation of labour. A century later, these would be applied rigorously for the first time to the manufacture of firearms.

Vauban believed in the possibility of 'escaping from chaos and confusion' through 'behaviour governed by calculation'. His concerns clearly went well beyond the battlefield. In the repeated journeys he undertook to inspect fortified towns and armies he acquired a stereoscopic vision of the realm and was, in fact, one of the few advisors of Louis XIV who had actually travelled it widely. He worried about obstacles to the circulation of goods and manpower, in particular the poor condition of routes and rivers. He showed the same concern about the number of customs stations and sought to 'relegate internal customs stations to the borders'. Here again, he showed a preference for waterways, conducting a detailed inventory of France's rivers and attempting to calculate their degree of navigability. With the same aim of unifying the nation, Vauban developed a 'General and easy method for population census' and suggested a model form in table format. He tried to link the population census project to the issue of tax reform, a suggestion that was so bold as to bring him into disgrace. By the second decade of the eighteenth century, the first geographers and the first Ponts et Chaussées engineers, entrusted with the building and maintenance of bridges, roads, canals, rivers and ports, drawn from the corps of fortification specialists, began systematic mapping of French territory (Mattelart, 1994).

In Vauban's treatise on how to take and defend fortified towns, he referred to the 'branch system', another term for networks. Although he did not invent the word 'network', Vauban is indeed the one who introduced the reticular perspective into the vision of strategic use of territory. In his time, the network metaphor was confined to the language of medical experimentation. Around 1665, referring to the 'reticular body of the skin', the Italian anatomist and naturalist Marcello Malpighi (1628–94), a precursor of histology or the science of tissue, transposed the word, previously used to designate the warp of fabric, net or lace, to the field of anatomy. It was no accident that Vauban's biographer, Pierre-Alexandre Allent (1772–1837), who was an officer in the engineering corps, should have been the one to ratify the use of the word 'network' in an essay on military reconnaissance in 1802. In this work, the hydrological network was compared to the branching of a tree. Thus, strictly speaking, the term 'network' did not come into use in military language until war ceased to be an affair of strategic position and siege, with mass conscription during the French Revolution in 1793 and with the fundamental change brought about by moving warfare, in which parallel lines and columns form, disband and redeploy. Half a century later, the expansion of the railway would speed up these changes.

Inventing a universal norm

The geometrical utopia of the revolutionaries

A norm or standard is that which allows the parts to be integrated into a whole. Whether technical or behavioural, norms and procedures determine the criteria of organisational efficiency.

> A norm establishes what is normal on the basis of a normative decision. . . . From the standpoint of standardisation, there is no difference between the birth of French grammar in the seventeenth century and the introduction of the metric system at the end of the eighteenth century. Richelieu, the *Conventionnels* and Napoleon Bonaparte were the

successive instruments of the same popular demand. We began with grammatical norms and ended up with the morphological norms for the people and horses required for national defence, along with standards for industry and hygiene. (Canguilhem, 1966: 181)

The Enlightenment and the system

Denis Diderot and Jacques d'Alembert placed their grand project of a *Dictionnaire raisonné des sciences, des arts et des métiers*, also known as the *Encyclopédie*, under the auspices of Francis Bacon. In the entry for 'Art', they paid tribute to him for having braved the *non plus ultra* of the Ancients and glimpsed the limitless ability of science and technology to 'break through the columns of fatality'. By linking 'mechanical and practical arts' to philosophical principles, the encyclo- paedists' enterprise, which came to fruition in 1772, con- tributed to the advancement of new technologies and methods. In the entry for 'System', Diderot seized upon the metaphor of the 'automated machine to measure time', the *machina machinarum*, to define the concepts of organisation, function and complication or complexity. Under 'Farmers' and 'Grain', the philosopher-physician François Quesnay (1694–1774), leader of the physiocrats, laid the foundations for the science of political economy. He also published the 'Economic Table', the first geometrical representation of the circulation of wealth. The fluidity of the movement of goods and people, and hence of communication routes, became the symbol of a doctrine that can be summed up in the maxim: '*Laissez faire, laissez passer*'. The entry 'Pin', in which a philo- sopher details the eighteen operations required to produce one, was to spur Adam Smith to provide a theoretical framework for the concept of the 'division of labour', a central principle in his project of a liberal economy (Smith, 1930).

At the time, the analogy of the machine was used alternately with that of the living organism to define the concept of 'system': 'The individual body is a huge clock; the collective body, a machine whose organisation responds to a mechanism of the same nature,' wrote the physician-philosopher Julien Offroy de La Mettrie (1709–51) in *L'Homme-machine* (Man, a Machine) in 1747. This organic vision of social mechanisms refers to the new 'anatomy of power' that confirmed the growing importance of panoptic prison and surveillance technologies, namely a set of minute disciplinary procedures designed to control and measure individuals. Michel Foucault wrote: 'La Mettrie's *L'Homme-machine* is both a materialist reduction of the soul and a general theory of conditioning (*dressage*), at the centre of which reigns the notion of "docility", which joins the analysable body to the manipulable body' (Foucault, 1977: 136). Since 1738, the mechanical flute player, created by Jacques de Vaucanson (1709–82), has served as a mechanical representation of man-as-machine.

The term 'normal' was borrowed by the French revolutionaries in 1789 from the vocabulary of geometry and referred to the T-square and the level (Macherey, 1992). These two emblems of Equality are attributes of the goddess Philosophy, the incarnation of Reason. The term was first applied to France's newly created teachers' schools. The ideal of egalitarian 'levelling', or the equalisation of citizens, inspired the Declaration of Human Rights, the unification of the French language through elimination of local dialects, the adoption of the Civil Code and the introduction of a system of statistics. The same ideal governed the division of administrative territories into *départements* and the location of public schools. The revolutionaries themselves were divided over the construction of this latticework grid, conceived as a coherent, hierarchical space. Regarding the distribution of schools, for example, some mocked the 'mathematical rabies' afflicting the project authors and accused them of denying the reality of a landscape shaped by history. The 'geometrical utopia' was accused of being ignorant of life (Julia, 1981). In London, right from the start of the revolutionary process, the English conservative political thinker Edmund Burke drove the point home by challenging the new departmental division: 'It is boasted that the geometrical policy has been adopted, that all local ideas should be sunk, and that the people should no longer be Gascons, Picards, Bretons, Normans, but Frenchmen, with one country, one heart and one assembly. But instead of being all Frenchmen, the greater likelihood is, that the inhabitants of that region will shortly have no country. No man ever was attached by a sense of pride, partiality, or real affection, to a description of square measurement. He never will glory in belonging to Chequer No. 71, or to any other badge-ticket' (Burke, 1986: 315). This line of argument was ambivalent, because it also acknowledged the validity of liberal principles; in place of abstract regulation by numbers, Burke was, after all, vaunting the concreteness and spontaneity of the providential market. In *The Rights of Man*, published in 1791, Thomas Paine made this reply to the Englishman's tract: 'It is power, not principles, that Mr. Burke venerates.'

The French government decree imposing the decimal system of weights and measures represented a highly symbolic normative decision, since it ran openly against the grain of prejudices and traditions dating back to feudal times, when the lack of standard measurements was an instrument for commercial trickery, favouring the rich and powerful. The metre thus appeared as the fulfilment of the secular idea of openness in trade. Derived from Nature – Nature shared by everyone, as defined by the Enlightenment philosophers – the new unit of measurement was glorified as the fruit of emancipating reason. As the bearer of universal values, it was seen as bringing men closer together (Kula, 1984).

The age of probable history

The topic of a universal language returned to the agenda with the philosopher-mathematician Condorcet (1743–94) and his plan to develop a language offering 'geometrical certitude'. The language of signs he proposed had to be able 'to bring to bear on all the objects embraced by human intelligence, the rigour and accuracy required to make the knowledge of truth easy, and error almost impossible' (Condorcet, 1794: 293). This language would make broad use of charts, tables, methods of geometrical representation and descriptive analysis. Following in the footsteps of Francis Bacon, whom Condorcet invoked as his inspiration, he wrote *Fragment sur l'Atlantide*, a utopian vision of the organisation of a republic of scientists one of whose tasks was to 'establish a universal language'. The project was explicitly based on a new relationship to history, that is, a conception of history as necessity, closely related to the theory of the perfectibility of human society. In Condorcet's view, if a new theory of history had become possible, it was because, by making use of past experience, in other words by observing the frequency with which events occurred, it was now possible to predict the future, at least in probable terms. On the eve of the events of 1789, he extrapolated from the argumentation of the Swiss

Jacques Bernouilli (1654–1705) concerning the abstract logic of probability theory, to determine more equitable methods of election to courts of assizes and representative assemblies, and to predict these bodies' concrete decisions. The experiment convinced Condorcet that he had discovered the philosopher's stone of a moral and political science as 'precise and exact' as the physical sciences. The future was no longer a field wide open to exploration, but had instead become predictable. Long-standing certitudes founded on temporal cycles and the repetition of events began to lose their hold. Unlike the island of old-fashioned utopias, Condorcet's depiction of the future of humankind embraced the larger world outside, indeed the whole planet.

The birth of redemptive discourse on long-distance communication

Someone made a remark about the telegraph which seems to me infinitely correct, and which brings out its full importance, namely that, at bottom, this invention might suffice to make possible the establishment of democracy among a large population. Many respectable men, including Jean-Jacques Rousseau, thought that the establishment of democracy was impossible among large populations. How could such a people deliberate? Among the Ancients, all the citizens were assembled in a single place; they communicated their will. . . . The invention of the telegraph is a new factor that Rousseau did not include in his calculations. It can be used to speak at great distances as fluently and as distinctly as in a room. There is no reason why it would not be possible for all the citizens of France to communicate their will, within a rather short time, in such a way that this communication might be considered instantaneous.

The foregoing text dates from March 1795 and was written by a man of science, Alexander Vandermonde

(1735–96), who held the first chair of political economy created in France. In August 1794, the Ministry of War opened the first optical telegraph line (Paris–Lille).

This prophetic discourse on the democratic virtues of long-distance communication would soon be contradicted by the continuation of the embargo on codes and encrypted 'languages of signs' and by the refusal to authorise their use for civilian purposes in the name of domestic security and national defence. This situation was to continue almost up to the arrival of the electric telegraph. No one but the person who transmitted the original and the final receiver knew the keys to the code formulated by the inventor of this technique, Claude Chappe. A star- or pyramid-shaped model would be used for the architecture of the network, which branched out from the top in Paris. Already employed for the national road network, it came into permanent use via the railroad and all later telecommunications networks.

Each new generation of technology revived the discourse of salvation, the promise of universal concord, decentralised democracy, social justice and general prosperity. Each time, the amnesia regarding earlier technology would be con-firmed. All these methods – from the optical telegraph to underwater cable, the telephone, the radio, the television and the Internet – intended to transcend the spatial and temporal dimensions of the social fabric, brought back the myth of the recovery of the lost agora of Attic cities (Mattelart, 1994, 1999). Neither the often radically different historical conditions of their institutionalisation, nor the flagrant failure to fulfil their promises regarding their sup-posed benefits, could make this millenarian world of tech-nological images falter.

In the early days of the Enlightenment, the quarrel between the Ancients and the Moderns had already begun to transform the historical view of the process by which modernity took shape. The habit of viewing universal history in terms of ages, and hence of giving succinct names to present and future society, did not develop until the end of the eighteenth century, although there were illustrious precursors such as Giambattista Vico (1668–1744) or the physiocrat Anne Robert Turgot (1727–81). In a speech delivered at the Sorbonne entitled *Tableau philosophique des progrès successifs de l'esprit humain* (A Philosophical Portrait of the Successive Advances of the Human Mind), Turgot had indeed anticipated this practice by outlining the progress of knowledge in three phases: theological, metaphysical and scientific. He insisted on the decisive role of tools of communication – language, writing and printing – in the configuration of different types of society epitomising various stages along the path of Enlightenment progress.

Condorcet, in turn, divided the methods of knowledge and their corresponding societies into historical periods in his *Esquisse d'un tableau historique des progrès de l'esprit humain* (Sketch for a Historical Picture of the Progress of the Human Mind), linking changes in transmission techniques to the shaping of institutions. He analysed the impact of printing on scientific development, the formation of democratic opinion and the growth of the ideal of equality. His vision of the benefits of communicating practical and theoretical knowledge and of increasing opportunities for scientific exchange, took the form of a determinist philosophy. Progress, characterised as an infinite, exponential process, was seen to accompany the irresistible ascension of the 'general illumination of minds'.

The 'romanticism of numbers', as the sociologist Max Weber called it, was to be put to the test by the pragmatic management of industrial society. People counted by numbers and, in the end, numbers alone would count.

2 Managing the Industrial and Scientific Age

The concept of industrialisation implies technology in tandem with organisation. There is a common theme linking the notion of the division of labour as developed by political economists, the principle of the division of mental operations underlying the mechanisation of thought, and the doctrine of scientific management of the workshop. Methods of governing were permeated by the idea that certitude lies solely in what can be counted. The notion of the 'average man', an emanation of probability theory, set the standard for the political management of crowds. Computer punch cards marked a decisive step in counting them. Each step in the progress of communication networks was accompanied by a utopia of universal community and decentralised society.

Towards a functional society

Society as industry

Before the process of industrialisation took shape in France, Claude Henri de Saint-Simon (1760–1825) developed a theory

of the role assigned to the organic alliance between manufacturers and 'positive scientists', in other words physiologists,
chemists, physicists and geometers (especially engineers from
the École des Ponts et Chaussées), in 'reorganising the body
politic' (Saint-Simon, 1821). In Saint-Simon's view, the only
way to overcome the crisis of civilisation was to treat society
like a large industry. The alliance between manufacturers and
positive scientists laid the foundation for a completely new type
of management, directed no longer towards the 'government of
men' but towards 'the administration of things'. The rise of a
technically trained elite would reduce the role of the state to that
of a mere chargé d'affaires or representative. A worldwide association of nations could come about only through the mediation
of the captains of industry. Such axioms concerning the 'industrial system' anticipated by nearly a hundred years the first
formulations of 'scientific management', one of the milestones
on the way to technocracy.

In Saint-Simon's view, the obvious failure of the French
Revolution was due to the fact that the culture of 'jurists',
'literati' and 'metaphysicians' had prevailed over the culture
of science. Their negative philosophy, essential during the
insurrectionary period of the Enlightenment, had proved harm-
ful when called upon to bind the will of the people to the project
of building new institutions. Only a positive philosophy would
be able to ensure the transition from the feudal, theological
age to the industrial, scientific age, and guarantee the passage
from a critical period to an organic or synthetic period. Saint-
Simon criticised Condorcet's theory of infinite perfectibility for
trusting too much in the harmonious evolution of progress and
overlooking the role of crisis and critical periods in social transformation. He nevertheless conceded that Condorcet could not
have avoided that pitfall, because his conceptual framework

was still weighed down by the methods of social mathematics and physics.

The project of building a 'science of man', to which Saint-Simon devoted himself in the early nineteenth century, drew from the new scientific perspective introduced by Xavier Bichat (1771–1802). By posing the constitution of living organisms as an object of knowledge, Bichat's work on the physiology of tissue sketched the outlines of a biological paradigm. It was no accident that Saint-Simon placed his intellectual project under the auspices of the neologism 'social physiology' and held that the 'industrial system' was configured like an 'organism', or better still, like a network-organism (Mattelart, 1994, 1999; Musso, 1997). The structural principle underlying the 'social organism' of the positive or industrial age was the hierarchy of functions. The network, whether material or immaterial and whether it involved transport or banking or functioned as a vector of symbols, was the archetype of organisation. Yet, Saint-Simon insisted, social reorganisation cannot fully succeed without a new religion, a 'new Christianity'. His initial theory of a functional, reticular society, revised and corrected by his disciples later on, drifted towards technological determinism. Michel Chevalier, a Saint-Simonian economist, would see as 'equivalent' the reduction of distances from one point to another and the elimination of class distinctions. Upon his return from a long study trip to the United States, he wrote: 'Thus, improving communications means working towards real, positive, practical freedom; it means allowing all the members of the human family to take part in the faculty of exploring and exploiting the planet which has been given to it as our heritage. . . . It means creating equality and democracy' (Chevalier, 1837: 31). Chevalier was one of the first French thinkers to manifest a fascination with the American model of domesticating space through networks. He also initiated the idea of combining the representation of the network with religious thought. In his *Dictionnaire de l'économie politique*, he noted: 'One could compare the zeal and ardour displayed by the civilised nations of today in establishing the railroads with what took place several centuries ago during the building of churches. . . . If, as we are assured, the word "religion" comes from *religare*, the railroads have more in common than we think with the religious spirit. There has never been such a powerful instrument for linking scattered peoples together' (Chevalier, 1852: 20). The era of activism in the Church of Saint-Simon had ended, and the doctrine of industrialism, a notion forged by Saint-Simon himself, was to lend legitimacy to the enterprising spirit of the builders of railroad and finance networks, shipping lines and inter-ocean canals.

In his youth, Auguste Comte (1798–1857), the founder of the discipline of sociology, supported Saint-Simon's attempt to explain the development of the industrial age, expressing his own theory of history as divided into three stages of knowledge: the early, primitive stage was dominated by theology; the second, a transitory stage, was dominated by metaphysics; the third and final stage was 'positive', dominated by science. Comte's 'three stages' of history was inspired by the intuitions of Turgot and Condorcet, but he kept his distance from the latter and his followers, whom he saw as relying too heavily on probability theory.

Against industrialism

'Industry has become the torture of peoples,' said Charles Fourier (1772–1837) in response to ardent supporters of industrialism. The utopian theorist of 'Universal Harmony' and the

'New Amorous World' could conceive of social reorganisation only as 'absolute separation' from the distorted world of 'Civilisation', a symptom of reason gone astray and the repression of human passion. Fourier's ideas concerning individual versatility, integral education and reconciling work with pleasure were to become key perspectives in the search for alternatives to the utilitarian mode of development, even though his central idea of restoring the world of passions was not always taken seriously.

Thomas Carlyle (1795–1881) embodied another facet of the critique of industrialism. In the work of this English writer and essayist, the attack on the harmfulness of the industrial age turned into nostalgia for an age of aristocracy of the mind and the cult of heroes. One might say that Fourier and Carlyle symbolised the two emblematic paths that would be adopted by those who criticised and resisted the culture of the industrial regime and its technical logics.

From the earliest days of the United States, the political question of the social project underlying the creation of the industrial system kindled passions in governmental spheres. Thomas Jefferson (1753–1826) was pitted against Alexander Hamilton (1757–1804), an advisor to George Washington, in a debate that still continues in today's digital era. Jefferson supported the model of decentralised society, which, anticipating the environmental movement, was based on giving autonomy to elected bodies at the local and regional levels and restricting the development of industry. He attempted to implement this model not only as a Democratic Party leader, in his successive roles as Vice-president and President, but also as an architect. Hamilton, on the other hand, advocated progress through the centralisation of power and by urban, industrial and financial concentration. Jefferson laid the foundations for a typically American tradition of radical criticism of the megalopolis, based on nostalgia for humanity's original relationship with the land – the virgin wilderness that characterised the heroic age of the pioneers. The tradition was carried on by Ralph Waldo Emerson (1830–82), in the form of a conception of democracy that exalted the ideal of individuals free from all constraints and able to do as they pleased. In 1865, Emerson described his disciples as 'Fanatics in freedom' who 'cannot tolerate any form of mediation'. At the dawn of the third millennium, the techno-libertarians of cyberspace, those fierce adversaries of the very idea of the nation-state, would draw on this tradition to justify their planetary project of 'virtual communities'.

Actuarial reasoning

The division of mental labour

As early as 1819, Charles Babbage (1792–1871) extended the concept of the division of labour to the operations of the mind. Adam Smith had limited the concept to mechanical operations within a factory, and failed to realise how much time could be saved in manufacturing by applying it to the organisation of mental labour. Babbage got the idea of extrapolating Smith's concept to intellectual operations by observing how Marie Riche de Prony (1755–1839), a French engineer from the École des Ponts et Chaussées, had gone about producing the tables of logarithms and trigonometry (to the 14th, 19th and 25th decimal places) required for calculating under the metric system. De Prony had indeed divided up the tasks into three 'workshops' with distinct functions. The first group, made up of five or six geometers, was in charge of finding simple formulae. The second group, composed of seven or eight mathematicians, translated these formulae into numbers. The last group, consisting of sixty to eighty calculators, 90 per cent of whom had only an elementary knowledge of the rules of arithmetic, performed the specified operations and drew up tables. Prony succeeded in filling seventeen large volumes with such tables.

The principle of the division of mental labour was the basis of Babbage's project to build a prototype of a calculating machine. Taking as his model the holes perforated in the boards of looms as vehicles for data, he first designed a 'difference engine' and then an 'analytical engine'. These 'number mills' which combined the whole range of available techniques (the steam engine, the windmill, programmed automata, mechanics), 'wove algebraic models the way a Jacquard loom weaves flowers and leaves,' according to Ada Augusta, Countess of Lovelace (1815–52), daughter of Lord Byron, to whom we owe one of the rare works describing the machines that was published during the inventor's lifetime.

Babbage also produced several works that help provide a historical context for his innovative approach. The first is dated 1826 and is concerned with a comparative study of life insurance establishments; this activity, even today, constitutes one of the privileged fields for applied mathematics. Indeed, his main reason for mechanising the processing of large series of numbers was to facilitate the calculation of insurance premiums by actuaries. The second work was a treatise in political economy concerning the mechanical arts, published in 1832 with the title *On the Economy of Machinery and Manufactures*. In his preface, the author described this work, a brilliant synthesis of the observations and studies he carried out in workshops and factories in England and on the Continent, 'as one of the consequences that have resulted from the Calculating-Engine, the construction of which I have been so long superintending'.

Indeed, he studied the various methods used to impose a hierarchy of operations and functions in the manufacturing process on workers: 'the master manufacturer, by dividing the work to be executed into different processes, each requiring different degrees of skill or of force, can purchase exactly that precise quantity of both which is necessary for each process' (Babbage, 1832: 175).

Babbage made no secret of his belief in the power of 'information machines'. He was, incidentally, one of the first to extend the use of the term to telegraph lines. Five years before the invention of the electric telegraph (1837), he predicted: 'These machines have generally been established for the purposes of transmitting information during war, but the increasing wants of man will probably soon render them subservient to more peaceful objects' (Babbage, 1832: 36).

In 1851, Babbage published a brochure on the Great Exhibition held at the Crystal Palace in London, an event that was singularly revealing. Proponents of free trade celebrated their victory over mercantilism, showcasing the free-market alternative to the nascent socialist doctrines expressed on the Continent during the revolutions that had been suppressed in 1848. The inauguration of the underwater cable linking Dover to Calais made this first link in a network intended to 'encircle the world' the symbol of the free-trade model of internationalisation. More prosaically, the organisation of the exhibits revealed the absence of a common criterion for classifying the 'works of industry of all nations'. Babbage's comments shed light on his belief in the virtue of 'information machines' as enabling the 'free and unlimited trade between nations' of knowledge as well as commodities. In his view, such trade could only 'contribute to the advantage and prosperity of all' (Babbage, 1851).

The average man, a unifying standard

Babbage, who held the chair once occupied by Newton at Cambridge, took advantage of the 1851 Exhibition to discuss the need to develop an official policy of support for technical innovation – a topic of special concern to him, since his inventions did not always earn the backing he wanted from the political sphere. He knew this demand could be satisfied only by allowing scientists themselves to take charge of organising exchanges at the international level. Outlining the recent history of such exchanges, he recalled that the first important assembly of European scientists, organised in Berlin under the presidency of Alexander von Humboldt, dated back only to 1828, and that some of those invited were unable to attend for want of an exit visa.

Babbage lent his support to the project of organising the first international statistics conference, proposed by the Belgian astronomer and mathematician Adolphe Quételet (1796–1874). This summit meeting of the community of statisticians, approved in principle at the end of the London event, was to take place two years later in Brussels. In addition to marking the first step towards setting international standards for nomenclature and methods of statistical observation, it offered the first example of a relatively stable network of scientific exchange.

Adolphe Quételet was the catalyst of actuarial reasoning. He acted as the ambassador for a model of organisation of statistics and census departments that he had created for the Belgian government in 1830, just after the country had gained independence. At the same time, he proposed a probability-based theory for ordering social action, leading to a new method for managing the *res publica*. What Quételet introduced as the new science of 'social physics' was based on the notion of the 'average person'.

'The man I am talking about here is society's equivalent to the centre of gravity in the human body; it is the average around which the components of society oscillate; he is, if you will, a fictional being to whom everything will happen in accordance with the average results obtained for society' (Quételet, 1835). The technology of risk developed by private insurance companies could be extrapolated to the social body as a whole. The application of probability theory thus opened the way to a new method of regulating society, namely the 'insurance society'; the underlying principle for the future welfare state and the institutional materialisation of the idea of mathematically calculated solidarity and interdependence (Ewald, 1986). The mean values extracted by the technology of risk from the distribution of statistical series (pertaining to population movements, criminality, suicide and other 'social facts') became norms of government. The statistical system provided a tool for the objective identification of 'disruptive forces' affecting the political system. 'Objective', in this case, meant not weighed down by the classical division resulting from value judgements distinguishing between good and evil.

In 1885, the International Institute of Statistics was set up, successfully crowning the strategy to create an organised scientific community foreshadowed by the 1851 Exhibition in London. Statistics had unquestionably come into favour. Some thought that the science of numbers was replacing history as a means of analysis, and even believed that this universal rationalisation announced the entry of humanity into a 'post-historical era' (Friedmann, 1949). In 1890, the federal government of the United States used the perforated card machine, invented ten years earlier by the statistician Hermann Hollerith (1860–1929), for the first time to process general census data. By 1896, the machine was being manufactured and marketed by Hollerith

Tabulating Machines Corporation, which later became IBM (International Business Machines).

Sciences based on the calculation of individual behaviour took off during the last two decades of the nineteenth century. After Quételet's bio-typology came anthropometrics, devised by Alphonse Bertillon, a doctor and the inventor of scientific police methods, who acknowledged the Belgian statistician as his *maître à penser* (Lanteri-Laura, 1970). Policemen, judges and forensic scientists were guided in their mission of social hygiene against the 'dangerous classes' by the use of nomenclature, indices and profiles. Machines for recording the pace of work in factories, stadiums and barracks provided knowledge that was helpful in maximising energy use. Few fields avoided control by figures: witness the French army intelligence department, implicated in the Dreyfus affair, which called itself the 'statistics department' (Canguilhem, 1966).

Taylor and Ford: the philosophy of Americanism

As early as the 1890s, Frederick Winslow Taylor (1856–1915) started recording the amount of time required for movement in the factory. Inspectors tracked the gestures of workers, using a 'watch book', that is, a chronometer hidden in a hollowed-out book. In 1911, the engineer distilled his experience in organising the division of labour into *Principles of Scientific Management*. (This happened to be the year in which time zones were aligned with Greenwich Mean Time to make time 'universal'.) The proponents of a free-market political economy consider this classic of scientific management the crowning point of a line of inquiry initiated by Adam Smith's *Wealth of Nations* and Charles Babbage's study of the manufacturing economy (Marshall, 1919). Starting in 1918, the leaders of the Soviet Union in turn declared their allegiance to the principles of Taylorism, after first declaring the 'science of the organisation of work' to be socially neutral. In other words, it was dissociated from its function in capitalist exploitation and enshrined as the prototype of rational organisation for socialist society as a whole. This was an early sign of the socialist leitmotif of the 'scientific and technological revolution'. Official Soviet doctrine never stopped proclaiming that this radical development could reach its culmination only in a socialist society, as the capitalist mode of production was tangled up in the anarchy of competition.

For market economies, there remained the task of formulating principles for the scientific management of consumption. In 1908, Henry Ford was able to put a modestly priced car on the market, and in 1913 he introduced assembly lines in his factories. Mobilisation for war delayed the application of Fordism as an all-encompassing mode of social regulation. During the 1920s, marketing techniques came into wide use as tools for managing mass consumption. Notions of opinion management and engineered consent began to circulate, pointing to an infatuation with the new method of governing mass democracy, involving a carefully calculated combination of information and censorship (Lippmann, 1922; Lasswell, 1927). Governments drew lessons from the intensive use of propaganda during the First World War. Theoreticians argued that the masses, as spectators of the action rather than as participants, had to be controlled for their own good by an intelligent minority, a class of specialists. The early formulation of global strategies in the Soviet Union and the Axis countries lent legitimacy to the enterprise of counter-propaganda. Opinion polls and surveys were part of the arsenal of New Deal measures to overcome the Depression. The mathematician Paul Lazarsfeld (1901–76), a pioneering figure in the functionalist sociology of the media, defended statistics as a scientific procedure and justified the application of social science to the demands of private enterprise. In 1939, Arthur Nielsen, who had invented the notion of market share during the 1920s, was the first to make use of the audiometer, an early instrument for measuring radio audiences.

In 1929, the Italian philosopher Antonio Gramsci interpreted 'Fordism' as an avatar of the 'philosophy of Americanism'. The new production method implied a complete way of life, a distinct way of thinking and feeling about life. Rationalising the system of production meant joining factory with society and private life with public life. Managerial monitoring of intensive labour on the assembly lines was combined with ideological control to be imposed on private life, the former being inconceivable without the latter. Gramsci took as an example the revival of puritanical sexual ideologies of the family that accompanied the 'new industrialism'. He also noted that the new mode of social regulation required the decline of critical or non-positivistic intellectuals. Only the 'organic intellectuals' of capitalism held sway in the society regulated by Taylorism and Fordism (Gramsci, 1971).

Taylor's fantasies of lobotomising the public, together with Ford's scientific approach to manufacturing, formed the backdrop for two dystopian visions: Yevgeny Zamyatin (1972, 1984) who foresaw the mechanisation of life, the engineering of people and the grip of great machines, whether through technology itself or the Great Machine of the State or Religion, and Aldous Huxley, author of *Brave New World* (1932) on Fordist society.

Charlie Chaplin's *Modern Times* was not far away. Speed had become the instrument of an obsession with productivism and with measurable human beings, who were subjected to a furious pace of work.

Prefiguring network society

The global city and the index card

In 1895 two pacifist lawyers, Paul Otlet and Henri La Fontaine, founded the International Institute of Bibliography in Brussels. Their aim was to build up a 'Universal Book of Knowledge' by 'recording on a day-to-day basis the intellectual work of both worlds'. For this new science of the systematic organisation of documentation, scientific publications were only components – chapters and paragraphs – of a vast documentary encyclopaedia encompassing the entire universe. Fifty years later, Jorge Luis Borges would describe the project as 'arbitrary imaginings', in the same category as the insane enterprise of a priori linguistic classification devised by John Wilkins in the seventeenth century. For specialists of information sciences, on the other hand, the initiative must be viewed as visionary; it was the forerunner of a new discipline (Bellardo and Buckland, 1998; Day, 2001).

In order to list this mass of writings and iconography, Otlet (1868–1944) perfected the system of universal decimal classification invented by the American Melvil Dewey in 1876 and adopted the standard index card (12.5 cm 7.5 cm). On the eve of the First World War, the Institute had already produced a Universal Bibliographic Repertory, a Universal Iconographic Repertory, a central catalogue of libraries, and International Documentary Archives, as well as established an international library and an international museum of documentary methods. Most importantly, the development of the Institute and the project of building a science of documentation went hand in hand with another initiative: the founding, in 1910, of a Central Office of the Union of International Associations, the official purpose of which was to develop a network of 'institutions, federations, leagues, congresses, institutes, commissions, standing committees, etc. created in the last fifty years' and to ensure the 'cooperation and coordination of efforts to unite all the individual systems of unification and units into one general system' (La Fontaine and Otlet, 1912).

The mission of the Central Office, 'to make the entire world into one city and all the people of the world into one family', reveals the political intuition underlying the creation of the Institute. Paul Otlet fought to give concrete form to his utopian global city or *mundaneum* in Brussels and Geneva by associating with architects such as Le Corbusier. Even more ambitious was his project for an 'Intellectual League of Nations' to offset the incompetence of the existing League of Nations (Otlet, 1919). Otlet coined the term *mondialisme* or 'worldism' to indicate more clearly the symbiosis of his project with the thinking of a universal network, at once technical and social. This thinking developed to the rhythm of a planet encircled by an underwater cable network, a universal post office and other technical networks as well as many networks of citizens that arose in the second half of the 19th century thanks to freedom of the press, expression and association, which gave an unprecedented impetus to exchange between civil societies. Otlet shared with

Gabriel Tarde, the pioneer of social psychology, whom he invoked to lend legitimacy to his great project, the conviction that the accelerated pace of information and communication flows in the nineteenth century had already generated a world-wide opinion and that the emergence of the modern 'public' was the outcome of means of communication that were constantly widening the 'social circle' above and beyond 'the barriers erected by clans, classes, denominations and the state . . . to the limits of the human species' (Tarde, 1890). Tarde chose the 'brain' as the analogue of modern society, unlike Herbert Spencer and Émile Durkheim, who preferred to conceive of society as an 'organism'. In Tarde's view, social systems did not evolve from a homogeneous to a heterogeneous state or from 'mechanical solidarity' to 'organic solidarity', but tended to develop in the opposite direction. The process of unifying multiplicity took place gradually and therefore difference remained the alpha and omega of the universe.

Contrary to the belief arising from a fascination with network society today, the reticular representation of the world came into being well before what is commonly called the 'information revolution'. The concept of 'network' had been associated in the past with the biomorphic notion of interdependence, borrowed from the language of cells. It is hardly surprising that, some forty years after founding the Bibliographical Institute of Brussels, Otlet anticipated the idea of a network of networks. In his principal legacy, *Traité de documentation, le livre sur le livre* (Treaty on Documentation: The Book About the Book), he presented the architecture of a 'universal network of information and documentation', linking production centres, distributors and users in every field and in every location. This great library would be equipped with screens. Thanks to the electric telescope, people would be able to access books by telephone and 'read pages at home requested in advance from books on display in the "teleg" rooms of major libraries' (Otlet, 1934).

Post-industrial decentralisation

Saint-Simon's philosophy of networks remained rooted in a centralising conception of social reorganisation. Anti-authoritarian movements countered it with a project for a 'society in which the centre would be nowhere and the circumference everywhere'. Two themes – dissolution of the city and dissolution of the state – were combined in anarchist theories from their inception, in the second half of the eighteenth century, and in particular with the publication in London in 1793 of the *Enquiry Concerning Political Justice and its Influence on Morals and Happiness* by William Godwin (1756–1836). In Godwin's project for society, individuals moved by reason to free themselves would settle in small communities without laws or fixed institutions. Pierre Joseph Proudhon (1809–65) would later redefine the project in his own way, in a movement that accompanied the rise of working-class organisations and struggles.

With the introduction of electricity, anarchist geographers combined Proudhon's principle of decentralised organisation of community associations with the free federation of free industrial and farming associations. This was the direction taken by the thought of the Russian philosopher Piotr Kropotkin (1842–1921) in the 1880s. In his view, the new form of energy signalled the death warrant of 'paleo-technical' civilisation. That civilisation, founded on the railway, steam energy, mechanics and networks of heavy industry, had resulted in a concentration of the means of production and in the crowded conditions in large urban centres. Entry into the neo-technical era meant releasing the potential for flexibility and ubiquity inherent in electricity. Taking decentralisation as its key principle, a new society would appear in which territorial imbalances would be corrected along with social ones. The neo-technical era would usher in the law of 'mutual aid' and 'mutual support' which Kropotkin thought was just as strong as the law of the survival of the fittest and which, he believed, had solidified the resistance of the people at the bottom of the social scale in the course of history. It would do away with the historical sources of injustice and inequality, including the international division of labour and the hierarchical opposition between city and country, industry and agriculture, intellectual and manual labour, and between work and leisure (Kropotkin, 1912). The 'mutualist' mode of organisation, the fruit of a new type of social contract spontaneously adopted at every territorial level by free and equal individuals, would render the state obsolete. Kropotkin's conception of social emancipation through neo-technical development would attract geographers and regional planners in search of an alternative model for land use, especially in England and the United States.

In 1913, the term 'post-industrial' was coined by the English-trained Indian scholar Ananda K. Coomaraswamy, a specialist in Far Eastern art and author of a seminal work on Buddhism and Hinduism. The notion carried with it the hopes of those who believed in the imminent collapse of industrial civilisation and a return to decentralised society. Coomaraswamy's originality lay in linking the idea of post-industrial society to the ideal of rediscovering the cultural diversity threatened by the centralising, standardising practices of a 'mechanical unit system' in the grip of an economy with planetary ambitions and totally lacking in concern for the 'soul of the species' (a theme that the canonical figures of the Indian Renaissance, from Tagore to Sri Aurobindo, held dear).

In 1917 the term 'post-industrial' was taken up by the Englishman Arthur J. Penty, a militant in the Socialist Guild, an admirer of William Morris' utopia, and a sharp critic of faith in the machine (Penty, 1917, 1922). Five years earlier, Hilaire Belloc, a Frenchman who had become an English citizen, had published his highly successful essay *The Servile State*, which crystallised criticism of the state. Although the use of the term 'post-industrial' remained relatively restricted, the philosophy underlying it continued to fuel a wide range of protests and movements opposed to the ravages of global development. The neologism resurfaced in the 1960s in a totally different ideological context.

In 1934, Lewis Mumford (1895–1990) took up the thread of Kropotkin's intuitions and updated them to include broadcasting networks. In his classic work *Technics and Civilization*, the American historian noted: 'Plato defined the limits of the size of a city as the number of citizens who could hear the voice of a single orator: today those limits do not define a city but a civilisation. Wherever neo-technic instruments exist and a common language is used, there are now the elements of almost as close a political unity as that which was once possible in the tiniest cities of Attica' (Mumford, 1934: 241). Even as utopias of communication were being revived, a philosophy of networks was being consolidated in the United States, with a strong link between the history of transmission techniques and that of institutional forms.

The architect of the Chicago School, Frank Lloyd Wright (1869–1959), combined Kropotkin's socialist-inspired thesis with the liberal philosophy of Jefferson and Emerson, thereby helping to blur traditional political divergence on the issue of decentralisation. His concept of 'organic space' resulted in a centreless topography of small, scattered units that were nevertheless linked to each other by a tight mesh of networks of circulation. It was a form of settlement designed to preserve individuality while creating a new type of sociability.

In Europe, the philosophy of Americanism confronted another utopia, the pedagogical project of generalised intellectual enlightenment inherited from the philosophers of the 18th century, which began to come under attack. The ideal of achieving democracy by gradually extending the values of high culture was challenged by the project of mass democratisation through cultural products circulated by the techno-mercantile system.

3 The Emergence of Computers

With the intense mobilisation of scientific resources, the development of computers made a decisive take-off during the Second World War. By the end of the conflict, three questions had emerged regarding the status of the world of information technology. To what extent did the pattern of worldwide confrontation between East and West determine the geopolitical framework of technological innovation? What were the terms governing the debate on the prevailing notion of 'information'? What was the role of new digital memory technologies in the history of civilisations?

Geopolitical stakes: the bipolar constraint

Towards an automated battlefield

In 1936 the English mathematician Alan Turing (1912–54) formulated a new technological principle: the idea of a pre-recorded program and that of a table of statements describing the problem to be solved. His machine, which was capable of embodying any 'well-defined procedure', helped shape the idea of a 'universal machine'. In keeping with the discovery of the mechanisms of the human brain, it paved the way to building an 'electronic brain'. Once the war had begun, the forerunners of future data-processing machines and theories became an integral part of the war effort. Progress in the development of large-scale calculators came from three directions: the decoding of strategic enemy correspondence, the improvement of anti-aircraft artillery, and the atom bomb (the Manhattan Project). Thus, as early as 1939, Alan Turing was recruited by the British Intelligence Service to crack the secret of the Enigma electromechanical coding machines developed by the Germans during the period between the wars. In the United States, Claude Elwood Shannon, a researcher at Bell Laboratories, also tackled the problem of codes, while the cybernetic expert Norbert Wiener worked on the ballistic missile project. All the American projects came under the umbrella programme of the US National Defense Research Committee, headed by Vannevar Bush, who had invented the first complete analogical calculator, the differential analyser, in the early 1930s.

In 1947, the US National Security Act revived the model of synergy among scientists, the private sector and defence needs already tested against the Axis powers. This time, it sought to unite the players involved in technological innovation against an enemy characterised as 'global', namely world communism. For the US government, this meant a significant institutional leap, whereas the Soviet state, which had considered itself a 'fortress under siege' from the very beginning, had remained in a state of mobilisation. The increasing flow of research and development contracts from the Pentagon, and later on from NASA (founded in 1958), fuelled the growing military-industrial complex. In 1930, the federal budget contributed 14 per cent of the financing of private and public research; by 1947 the figure had risen to 56 per cent. By 1965, 88 per cent of the research funds devoted to the aerospace industry and 60 per cent of electronics came from the government (Mattelart, 1976). The first major achievement of this strategy, designed to meet the threat of nuclear war, was the inauguration of SAGE (Semi-Automatic Ground Environment System), an air defence system, by the US Air Force in 1955. The architecture of SAGE prefigured the large systems of real-time connection between computers. It was the first complete circuit of detection, decision and retaliation. The system was designed to link together radar equipment installed along US borders, interpret their signals and direct aircraft to intercept the enemy target. SAGE was more than a weapons system; it was 'a dream, a myth, a metaphor for total defence' (Edwards, 1989). Other detection systems were to follow at a frantic pace: the BMEWS (Ballistic Missile Early Warning System), the DEW (Distant Early Warning) and the SACCS (Strategic Air Command Control System).

The omnipresent role of the Strategic Air Command (SAC) in orienting research and development testifies to the tenacity of the doctrine, which grew up during the war, that air power determines the outcome of war (MacIsaac, 1986). The first argument in favour of aviation was its inherent flexibility. Secondly, as war increasingly became an 'industry in itself', only air power could manage it efficiently, and at lower cost in human lives. This latter aspect was also a way of guarding against an unfavourable reaction from American public opinion, which tended towards pacifism. The ideal of automated battle management arose in this context (Barnaby, 1986). Information engineers began developing their own discourse on systems, communication and control. The computer acquired its true meaning as a 'universal machine' 'theoretically able to solve any problem that could be formulated precisely enough – that is, that could be systematized, mathematized, modelled, reduced to an algorithm' (Edwards, 1989: 149). Information technology in itself became the first theoretician of air power. This ideology, bearing the stamp of technological determinism, would henceforth support the embedding of artificial intelligence in weapons systems.

Operations research and think tanks

During the Second World War, the term 'Operations Research' was used to describe research aimed at developing a 'formalised scheme for applying quantitative analysis to military operations' (Dickson, 1971: 22). In addition to the ties of ongoing cooperation between civilian and military and between private and public research, a new link was created in the chain of production of operational knowledge: think tanks. At the outset, these new research institutions were staffed by demobilised engineers and scientists. The first and most famous think tank was Rand (Research And Development Corporation), founded in 1946 by the US Air Force in Santa Monica, California. This idea factory, which would later include a centre of higher learning, was the birthplace of systems analysis, cost-effectiveness methods and the Planning, Programming and Budgeting System or PPBS, as well as game theory applications. Specialists in the social sciences, economists, mathematicians, engineers and physicists were invited to pool their knowledge, as they had during the war. Originally founded as a department of Douglas Aircraft Company, Rand became a separate entity two years later and adopted the status of a 'non-profit independent enterprise'. A new function came into being: the military intellectual, a consulting expert who could 'move freely through the corridors of the Pentagon and the State Department rather as the

Jesuits through the courts of Madrid and Vienna three centuries ago' (Bell, 1962: 33).

Norbert Wiener: the humanist promise against the current

In 1948, Norbert Wiener (1894–1964) published *Cybernetics or Control and Communication in the Animal and the Machine*. The book, which combined the observation of physiological and neuro-physiological processes (heart muscle contraction and nervous system performance seen as integral wholes) with a general theory of technological control systems, was the starting point of the 'science of steering' or cybernetics. The name was chosen with reference to the automatic governor of ships, one of the first devices able to 'think by itself', and one of the first and best-developed forms of feedback. In cybernetic thinking, causality is circular. Intelligence does not radiate from a central decision-making position at the top, where information converges and from which decisions are disseminated through a hierarchy of agents, but rather involves an organisation or system of decentralised, interactive control.

Wiener postulated that information, with its potential to de-concentrate and decentralise, would be the origin of a 'Second Industrial Revolution', bearing the promise of freedom for the citizenry. Abandoning the strictly statistical definition of the notion of information, he extended it to include all 'means for the acquisition, use, retention, and transmission of information: the press, both as it concerns books and as it concerns newspapers, the radio, the telephone system, the telegraph, the post, the theatre, the movies, the schools and the church'. Yet the hopes he placed in communicating machines were accompanied by serious reservations. To thwart entropy, information had to be able to circulate without any impediments. In contemporary society, however, the game of power and money is an obstacle to the free flow of information and 'of all the anti-homeostatic factors in society, the control of the means of communication is the most effective and most important' (Wiener, 1948: 160). In order to find a system of moral values capable of releasing the liberating potential of information, it was first necessary to avoid thinking exclusively in terms of buying and selling and worshipping the 'fifth power' – the market. Wiener was concerned not only about the trend towards monopolisation and commodification of information sources, but also about the instrumentalisation of science for military ends.

> A certain blend of wheedling, bribery, and intimidation will induce a young scientist to work on guided missiles or the atomic bomb. To determine these, we have our machinery of radio fan ratings, straw votes, opinion samplings, and other psychological investigations, with the common man as their object; and there are always the statisticians, sociologists, and economists available to sell their services to these undertakings. Luckily for us, the merchants of lies, the exploiters of gullibility, have not yet arrived at such a pitch of perfection as to have things all their own way. (Wiener, 1948: 160)

Wiener belonged to a generation convinced of the need for welfare state policies, which, in his view, had proven effective during the New Deal. He thought that only Keynesian economics could control the anti-homeostatic factor contained in the logic of the market. He believed in the salutary mission of science and scientific thinking: new knowledge had to ensure that humanity did not plunge once again into the 'world of Belsen and Hiroshima', of concentration camps and nuclear annihilation. At the same time, his scepticism kept him from sharing the mystique of infinite progress that led Vannevar Bush in 1945 to submit a report to the President of the United States entitled *Science: The Endless Frontier*. In it, Bush proposed a programme of massive state aid to research and education with a view to hastening the advent of a 'post-historic' age. The Cold War caused this idea to be shelved and forgotten.

In April 1951, Univac I, the first computer intended for non-military use, was delivered to the US Bureau of the Census.

This type of all-round, interdisciplinary think tank gradually came to be seen as a strategic place for producing the knowledge required to plan the society of the future. The contract awarded to Rand in 1946 by the US Air Force to study the possibilities of satellites and space exploration, entitled *Preliminary Design of an Experimental World-Circling Spaceship* was revealing in this regard. When the Rand Corporation took out a patent in the 1950s on a forecasting technique called 'Delphi', it lent legitimacy to the idea that there were objective methods for exploring the future. The procedure consisted first in asking a sample group of experts to make forecasts about a specific issue. In the second phase, the replies (anonymous and sent by post) were sent back to the same experts, who could then compare their own forecasts with those of their colleagues, to see whether they had been invalidated or confirmed. The forecast approach did not come into its own until the following decade. Technological forecasting directly benefited from the research carried out for the Strategic Air Command, resulting in a qualitative leap in techniques, including the extrapolation of trends, the so-called 'relevance tree' method using graphs, the study of the diffusion times of technologies, morphological research, and so on.

In 1958 – a crucial year if ever there was one, since the Soviet Union had challenged the United States the previous year by launching its satellite, Sputnik, thereby opening another front for the Cold War: the struggle for the conquest of space – the Pentagon set up an agency to coordinate federal research contracts, the DARPA (Defense Advanced Research Projects Agency). Ten years later, this agency introduced the network Arpanet, an ancestor of the Internet, to facilitate the exchange of information between teams working on research contracts. In this 'republic of computer engineers', dependent on government contracts and sheltered from the outside world, the idea arose that the model of sociability developed around and through the Arpanet could be applied in the ordinary world. According to Patrick Flichy, 'They thought that the principles of egalitarian exchange and the free and open circulation of information within a cooperative network run by its users who made up the core of the academic Internet would circulate along with the new technology' (Flichy, 1999: 113).

Until the end of the 1950s, contracted research was geared to meeting the demands engendered by the doctrine of nuclear dissuasion and of massive counter-strikes, namely, confrontation with the Communist enemy. The Kennedy administration was to change all that. The doctrine of 'limited warfare', developed in response to guerrilla warfare in third world countries, defined other needs arising from so-called counter-insurgency strategies. In the area of technological innovation, emphasis was placed on developing new surveillance and reconnaissance devices, counter-infiltration alarms, sensor-aided detection systems (olfatronic and infrared, acoustic and seismic), radio communications, computers and satellite connections in the field. In short, the microtechnologies of the electronic battlefield began to emerge (Klare, 1972). As for strategic analysis, social systems engineering provided the criterion for information gathering with a view to developing models to simulate 'operations'. Social scientists were expected to explain insurgent behaviour and build analytical models of social change and social control in order to turn civilian populations away from the temptation to resort to violence. They were also expected to propose ways of improving the interface between man and machine. This redeployment called for a restructuring of the state – a rationalising task assigned to Robert McNamara from 1960 to 1965, when he imposed management methods on the Pentagon and set up an Office of Systems Analysis. He entrusted the job to Rand experts who introduced the Planning, Programming and Budgeting System (PPBS), forcing planners to rationalise their budgets in accordance with long-term political objectives. During the Second World War, McNamara, who trained as a mathematician, had developed systems analysis techniques for the Statistical Control Office of the US Air Force. When John Kennedy appointed him Secretary of Defense, he was not only teaching at Harvard Business School, but was also the chairman and CEO of the Ford Motor Company. When he completed his stint at Defense, he was named president of the World Bank, where he remained until 1981.

At the diplomatic level, after the Second World War, the State Department set about trying to convince United Nations bodies of the legitimacy of its doctrine of the free flow of information, which was increasingly assimilated to that of free trade. It opposed this doctrine to that of the Kremlin, which was tethered to the thesis of national sovereignty and viewed any spilling across borders as 'interference' or 'aggression' (Schiller, 1976; Mattelart, T., 1995). In 1965, Washington offered the 'free world' countries Intelsat (International Telecommunications Satellite Consortium), the first communication system with global coverage and a model of informational opulence. In the early 1970s, with the end of the space race and US–Soviet *rapprochement* through *détente*, the conversion of technology to civilian purposes provided the basis for the 'revolution in communications' slogan invented by Madison Avenue advertisers. As for the USSR, boxed into its model of social control based on information scarcity, its electronic industry would continue to be used essentially for defence purposes.

The scientific stakes: the definition and measurement of information

The mathematical theory of communication

In 1949, the engineer and mathematician Claude Elwood Shannon (1916–2001) first formulated a mathematical theory of communication. His definition of information was strictly statistical, quantitative and physical. It referred primarily to 'quantities of information', disregarding the etymological root of the word 'information', which denotes the process whereby knowledge is given form by the structuring of fragments of knowledge (MacKay, 1969; Dubos, 1970). The problem posed had to do with calculating probabilities: the key was to find the most efficient, in other words the fastest and least expensive, system for coding telegraphic messages from a transmitter to a receiver. The mechanical model, concerned solely with the communication channel, reflected a behaviourist or stimulus–response conception of society and was perfectly consistent with a model of infinite progress disseminating from the centre to the peripheries. The receiver was doomed to be, as it were, a clone of the transmitter. The construction of meaning had no place in Shannon's research programme. The notion of communication was thus severed from the notion of culture. As one specialist in cultural studies noted, this approach to communication reflected a particular representation of American society, the concept of culture being 'a weak, evanescent notion in American social thought' (Carey, 1975). This sense of the term 'communication' soon became widespread.

As for the notion of 'information', it was rapidly transformed into a black box, that is, an all-purpose keyword, a genuine 'semantic Proteus' released from the 'Pandora's box of fuzzy concepts' (Thom, 1974). This was made all the easier by the fact that many disciplines in the human sciences, eager to share in the legitimacy of the natural sciences, raised Shannon's theory to the level of a paradigm.

An accounting matrix

The first attempt to quantify the activities of information production and distribution was made in 1962 by Fritz Machlup (1908–83), an American economist known for his work on technological innovation and the balance of payments. Machlup did not try to hide the marginal uncertainty surrounding this type of enterprise, and thus showed considerable epistemological caution. What is striking today is the modesty with which he stated the practical aim of his research: to provide a basis for thinking about reforming education and training systems, one of the major objectives of his study being to measure their productivity. There is no trace of any prophesying regarding the advent of a new knowledge society. His attitude contrasted sharply with the intellectual and political environment of the following decade, when the question of measuring information became part and parcel of the debate over the 'information age' and the coming of the 'information society'. This thesis gained currency in 1977 with the publication of a nine-volume study on the definition and measurement of the 'information economy', carried out at the request of the United States government by the Franco-American economist Marc Uri Porat.

Starting from an open-ended conception of the information spectrum, Machlup had avoided reducing information to activities involving the intensive use of technology and in fact raised the question of non-industrial practices. Porat, on the other hand, focused on information systems (computers and telecommunications), and the resulting definition of information was in line with the pure statistical tradition: 'quantities of data that are organised and communicated'. When he finished his inventory of national accounting, he classified 'information agents' into six sectors: industries selling information goods and services, public bureaucracy, private bureaucracy, the public production sector, private production activities and households. He arrived at the following conclusion: by 1967, information already accounted for 46 per cent of the gross national product of the United States and 53 per cent of all wages.

Structuralism and the cyberanthrope

'The short term is the most capricious and deceptive of all time periods,' wrote Fernand Braudel in the late 1950s in his critique of structuralist methods that drew on the information model. A structure, Braudel observed, is an architecture and a reality that time does not wear out but operates for a long period. Contemporary social life is made up of a collection of movements of various origins and paces (Braudel, 1958).

By aligning itself with information theory, structural linguistics – the trend-setting discipline of the 1960s – claimed to offer a model for the social sciences that would give them an identity as well as legitimacy close to those of the exact sciences. Language as a system defined society as a system. Molecular biology, which had just discovered the genetic material contained in DNA, shared a common conceptual topography with the structural analysis of discourse: codes, information systems, programmes, signs and messages (Jakobson, 1962; Jacob, 1970). The text was sovereign. A system of communication referred only to the laws of its own internal structure. A corpus was irreducibly closed in upon itself. Speakers and receivers of statements vanished, along with their interests.

Analogical transfer became the rule. In the field of urban development theories, for example, 'the city as an "advertising" and "self-advertising" structure, as a network of communications, became a sort of machine constantly emitting messages' (Tafuri, 1979: 145). This representation of the city as a programmed network of communications reflected the need for an integration plan. The concept of information overload was understood as an input of information into an urban system that exceeded the latter's capacity to process it efficiently: in other words, to translate it into decision-making without excessive mistakes, distortion or delay (Meier, 1962).

Henri Lefebvre, the philosopher of the city and of daily life, denounced the fetishism of information behind which 'panstructuralism' was hiding. The fantasy of an analogical language of information concealed the fact that intensified circulation of information merely brought a crowning touch to the cohesive, systemic role historically played by the circulation of money and material goods. It was, Lefebvre warned, a harbinger of the advent of a society managed by a 'new species' of 'cyberanthropes', who considered themselves, declared themselves and were indeed becoming global, and who diminished everything they touched, starting with social contradictions. The cyberanthrope resembled 'the last man' heralded by Nietzsche. He expressed 'the drying up of thought and of life'. 'The cyberanthrope has obviously grasped how the concepts of stability, equilibrium and self-regulation, which claim to be both practical and rational, can thus unite the ideal and the real. He has clearly understood how these concepts are linked to those of the Norm and the Rule. And of efficiency' (Lefebvre, 1967: 195). The only effective tactic for confusing the issues surrounding cyberanthropic order and balance was the 'fight of the retarius against the gladiator, the net against the sword'.

In *La Technique ou l'enjeu du siècle* (Technology or the Stakes of the Century), written in 1950 and published in 1954, Jacques Ellul was more sceptical about the possibilities of grassroots resistance to the irrepressible rise of a 'technological system' that had become autonomous, which he defined as totalising, universalising and self-reproducing. It was a 'new tyrant' that subordinated the system of nature and that of society to its particular criteria of efficiency. In Ellul's view, neither morality nor politics, which were increasingly reduced to techniques, appeared to be capable of orienting technological growth. Two full decades before the concern became meaningful to society, Ellul pointed to the keeping of computerised files on the population as a mechanism for neutralising any form of protest. His book was introduced to critics in the United States by Aldous Huxley, who recommended it for publication by the Center for the Study of Democratic Institutions at Santa Barbara. It was published in 1964 with the title *The Technological Society*, and soon became a standard work in the field (Christians and Real, 1979). Another important work by this pioneering and prolific author was *Propagandes* (Propaganda. The Formation of Men's Attitudes), published in 1962, which extended the analysis of the technological system to the media.

The important thing was that, henceforth, policymakers had a legitimate accounting matrix to draw upon (Porat, 1978). While Porat was still putting the final touches to his research report, it was already being used as the basis for an official document drafted in 1976 under the direction of Nelson Rockefeller, which laid down the outlines of a National Information Policy. The following year, the Organisation of Economic Cooperation and Development (OECD) invited Porat to build a model to classify its member countries on a scale leading up to the 'information society'.

Each new generation of computers contributed to the protean nature of information. The mixtures, overlappings and equivalences of knowledge and understanding, culture and communication grew to such an extent that the boundaries separating knowledge, understanding, culture and communication became increasingly blurred (Thayer, 1970; Rougemont, 1981; Wilden, 1987; Breton, 1987, 2000; Sfez, 1988). During the

1970s, sociologist Edgar Morin, explaining the notion of 'information', wrote that the knowledge, know-how, standards, norms, prescriptions and prohibitions making up culture constituted a genuine *génothèque** of human societies (Morin, 1974). A few decades later, the philosopher of technology, Bernard Stiegler, defined information as 'that which has value only because it loses it'. In other words, since the value of information is linked to the amount of time it takes to circulate, it is, by definition, a commodity consisting of perishable memory and opens up a new form of temporality in stark contrast to the time required for the creation of knowledge (Stiegler, 1991).

The fuzziness of the notion of information continued to surround that of the 'information society'. The early determination to give political legitimacy to the idea of such a society existing, here and now, overcame any misgivings prompted by epistemological caution. Information was increasingly assimilated to the statistical term 'data' and identified as such only where there was a technical apparatus to process it. Thus, a purely instrumental concept of the information society took hold. The social atopia and indeterminacy of the concept blurred the sociopolitical stakes underlying an expression that was supposed to designate the new fate of the world.

The weight of the knowledge industry

From the outset, Fritz Machlup refused to separate information from knowledge:

---

* This term is made up of *géno*, signifying the human species and *thèque*, the suffix of *bibliothèque*, meaning a library. The term thus designates a full record of human cultural accomplishment.

Linguistically, the difference between knowledge and information lies chiefly in the verb form: to *inform* is an activity by which knowledge is conveyed; to *know* may be the result of having been informed. 'Information' as the act of informing is designed to produce a state of knowing in someone's mind. 'Information' as that which is being communicated becomes identical with 'knowledge' in the sense of that which is known. Thus, the difference lies not in the nouns when they refer to *what* one knows or is informed about; it lies in the nouns only when they are to refer to the *act* of informing and the *state* of knowing, respectively (Machlup, 1962: 15).

By postulating that 'to produce knowledge' means not only adding to the sum total of what is known but also creating a state of knowledge in someone's mind, Machlup was able to nullify the linear axiom and open the way to a multilevel analysis of the actors (and the occupations) involved in building the process of information/knowledge. The 'producers of knowledge' or 'communicators' are indeed found at several levels: *transporters*, who relay messages without changing them; *transformers*, who modify the form (such as stenographers); *processors*, who change the form and content by limiting themselves to routine procedures of rearranging, combining and calculating (such as accountants drawing up a balance-sheet); *interpreters*, who act on the form and content (such as translators); *analysers of messages*, who combine established procedures with their personal contribution in such a way that the transmitted message bears little or no resemblance to the received message, and finally, *original creators*.

Machlup also developed a classification based on the type of knowledge or information, in which he distinguished five categories: practical knowledge, which is useful for work, decision-making and action (all the knowledge relating to professional life, business, politics, household management); intellectual knowledge (scientific teaching and general culture); knowledge acquired as a hobby or entertainment; spiritual knowledge linked to religion; and random knowledge, picked up by accident and poorly retained. At the conclusion of his analysis, Machlup attempts to estimate the weight of the knowledge industry in the US economy: between 1940 and 1959, the workforce employed in this sector in the United States grew by 80 per cent, compared to an average of 23 per cent for the rest of the economy. By 1960, it accounted for 29 per cent of the country's gross domestic product.

The civilisational stakes: a history of the logistics of thought

The determinist temptation

Every new medium brings with it a new civilisation. This powerful idea, contained in embryo in the work of Condorcet and Lewis Mumford, came to the fore in the 1950s.

The Canadian Harold Innis (1894–1952) attempted to show how the technology of communication determined the forms taken by power, especially the forms of imperial domination (Innis, 1950; 1951). Innis chose his own country, precariously located between the British empire with its time bias and the American empire with its space bias, as his object of study. The concept of a 'bias of communication' divided vectors of communication into those that were time-binding – the tradition of oral and written speech – and space-binding – the mechanised tradition represented by printing and electronic communication. Each of these tendencies has its own corresponding social configuration. The first tended towards decentralisation and emphasised memory, a sense of history, small communities and assemblies, and dialogic forms of power. The mechanised tradition, on the other hand, is centralising by definition and governs the expansion and control of territory. Relying on the dialectical process of centralisation and decentralisation, it strengthens the centre from the peripheries. Every step forward in the development of high-speed technologies of expression and transmission destroys components of the human community. Inequalities in the speed of communication lead to 'monopolies of knowledge' – another core concept – which are at once the instrument and the result of political domination. Thus, according to Innis, the true aim of the First Amendment of the US Constitution is to guarantee the protection of the 'monopoly of knowledge' exercised by the press. By establishing freedom of the press, the Constitution sacrificed the right of people to speak to each other and inform each other and replaced it with the right to be informed by others, particularly professionals.

Another Canadian, Marshall McLuhan (1911–80), summed up in a terse formula the primacy of communication technology in the shaping of civilisation: 'The medium is the message.' From this standpoint, the history of humanity can be divided into three periods: first, the age of natural communication, through speech and gestures, involving all the senses, which was an age of magic and tribalism; secondly, the age of the tyranny of vision, opened up by alphabetical writing and printing, which was a period of abstract rationalism and nationalism; thirdly, the age of electronic transmission, which established the return of the full range of the senses. This was an age of new tribalism – this time, on a planetary scale.

McLuhan acknowledged that his books were only a 'distillation' of the intuition of his fellow countryman, Innis. Yet, the differences between them are far from negligible. Innis was a geographer concerned with political economy, whose writings bore the stamp of academic research. Haunted by the spectre of fascism and a sense of injustice, he denounced contemporary forms of imperialism and the rise of large corporations. He tended towards atheism. McLuhan, on the other hand, was a specialist in Elizabethan literature, to which he devoted his doctoral thesis. He was a fervent convert to Roman Catholicism (Kerkhove, 1990). Alternately described as an artist whose jerky style was in keeping with electronic culture, and an object of exaggerated praise as well as criticism, and promoted to the status of best-selling author, he gave the impression, above all, of surfing over society and history. In postulating that the content of the message was indissoluble from its form, McLuhan took a position diametrically opposed to the distinction between the signifier and the signified advocated by structural analysis in its obsession with the text. The reconciliation of form and content promised by McLuhan was achieved, however, by giving the former a monopoly on the communication process.

Memory technologies

In 1964, the ethnologist and specialist in prehistory André Leroi-Gourhan (1911−86) brought out a two-volume work entitled *Le Geste et la parole* (The Hand and the Word). The first volume dealt with technology and language, and the second with memory and rhythm.

From oral literature to figuration in general to perforated cards and electronic memory, the 'anthropian' (the human being) was gradually led to delegate the faculty of recording knowledge, the group's intellectual capital, to artefacts or artificial organs. The transmission of these 'series of programmes' was the necessary condition for material and social survival. Like tools, human memory is externalised. It was this history of collective memory that Leroi-Gourhan recounted as a 'transmission of programmes' spread out over five periods, marked successively by oral transmission, written transmission with tables and an index, simple index cards, mechanical reproduction and finally, electronic seriation.

Leroi-Gourhan made use of a broad concept of memory, which, in whatever forms it took, could be seen as the 'medium in which a chain of actions is inscribed'. He spoke of a 'specific memory' that reflects fixed behaviours of animal species; an 'ethnic memory' that ensures the reproduction of behaviour in human societies; and an electronic, 'artificial memory' that 'ensures the reproduction of a chain of mechanical actions without recourse to instinct or reflection'. The idea of mechanically performing a series of technical gestures slowly developed over the course of history. From the beginning of hominisation, the hand, language and the sensorimotor cortex formed the triangle around which the history of the organisation of collective memory and the externalisation of human organs revolved. The tool truly exists only in the 'gesture that makes it effective' and the synergy that takes place between them presupposes a memory in which the programme of behaviour is inscribed. The production of automatic programmes is a culminating point in human history, as important as the development of tools for chopping and striking (contemporaneous with the hammer, the club and the spatula) or of agriculture. The patient evolution of the tools of memorised gestures constitutes the human adventure of 'planetisation'.

The religion of the infosphere

McLuhan was the first to update the old dream of a pre-Babel humanity for the electronic age, a feat he accomplished with his first bestseller *The Gutenberg Galaxy* (1962), in which he unveiled the notion of the *global village*. The notion introduced 'global' vocabulary, hitherto reserved for military strategy, into the sphere of civilian life. It was fated to turn into a cliché by coming into worldwide use, particularly from the 1980s onwards. McLuhan was the first sorcerer's apprentice of techno-global symbolics, which explains why other inventors of neologisms pertaining to future society always position themselves in relation to this shock formula. He was also among the first to create a bridge between the videosphere and the infosphere, particularly in the last chapter of *Understanding Media* (1964). Finally, and decisively, McLuhan, a Toronto professor, reconstructed a religious vision of planetary integration applicable to every stage of the information age, regardless of the technological generation. Through him, theology became the cult of networks.

McLuhan's work combines various intellectual influences. These include, of course, Harold Innis, but also the ideas of Kropotkin and Mumford regarding the potential of electric networks to recreate community, although his references to these authors come close to a caricature of their thought. 'Electricity', he writes, 'does not centralize, but decentralizes. It is like the difference between a railway system and an electric grid system: the one requires railheads and big urban centers. Electric power, equally available in the farmhouse and the Executive Suite, permits any place to be a center, and does not require large aggregations' (1964: 36). Finally, there is the relation between McLuhan the convert and the work of the Jesuit theologian and palaeontologist Pierre Teilhard de Chardin, from whom he borrowed his eschatological vision of the 'noosphere' and 'planetization', that is, the inclusion of 'humanity as a whole' under the combined influence of communication machines and 'overheated Thought' to produce 'the Spirit of the Earth, the synthesis of individuals and peoples, the paradoxical conciliation of the element with the whole, and of unity with multitude'. Through the connectivity and density of communication networks, the whole of humankind is entering the last stage of human life (*hominisation*): the spiritualisation of the world. This movement away from the aggressive power of empires means the advent of a 'new world of consciousness', with 'our power of loving developing until it embraces the total of men [*sic*] and of the earth' (Teilhard, 1959: 265). This influence was premonitory, for in the age of cyberspace, the works of Teilhard de Chardin were to become the 'little red book' of many of the techno-libertarian faithful.

McLuhan's writings closely mirrored the events of his time. First, they reflected the story of the conquest of space, a symbol of the accomplishment of the myth of the 'great human family', which began with the launch of Sputnik on 17 October 1957. According to McLuhan, this date marked the first time the planet earth was grasped as a 'global stage' in which the spectators have turned into actors. The Vietnam War, on which he performed a 'mediological' autopsy, gave him an occasion to put the finishing touches to the notion of the global village. It was the first war to be broadcast live, allowing audiences to 'take part from their living rooms', and demonstrated the power of electronic images to make history and make peace. A 'genuine planetary communism' was coming into being, he predicted, far more real than the one displayed in worldwide communist propaganda. Society would no longer be divided into military and civilian spheres, and the sources of conflict in the third world would fade away as it swiftly closed the gap separating it from the industrialised countries in terms of electronic technology. Third world countries, which McLuhan saw as still close to an oral, tribal culture, would be in the best possible position to take advantage of the new planetary electronic tribalism and the return to the full range of the senses (McLuhan and Fiore, 1968).

This egalitarianism, with its air of determinism, ignored the mechanisms of unequal exchange and underestimated the complexity of culture. The 'One World' of the global network forestalled the subversive force of the anti-industrialist utopia, which the early thinkers of the electric network envisioned as the potential basis for a more just society. All protest against 'monopolies of knowledge' vanished. Just as McLuhan's idealism was gaining strength in the media, Lewis Mumford, who no longer shared the prophetic belief in the saving virtues of artefacts of instantaneous communication and data storage systems, condemned 'technological compulsiveness' and predicted the reign of the 'Megamachine' and of 'Organisation Man'. The panoptic eye of the computer was taking the place of God (Mumford, 1967, 1970).

The British anthropologist Jack Goody also re-examined the question of the medium in *The Domestication of the Savage Mind* (1977). He wrote: 'Even if the message cannot reasonably be reduced to the medium, any change in the system of human communication must have great implications for the content'

(Goody, 1977: 9). He illustrated this with an analysis of the effects of writing on 'modes of thinking' (or cognitive processes).

Once the seminal contribution of the civilisational perspective to thinking about technologies of memory — and more generally about the question of the medium — has been recognised, the next step is to subject it to socio-political analysis. Indeed, in every civilisation, each time and place forges its own method of appropriating and incorporating technology, thereby producing a plurality of communicational configurations with their various levels — economic, social, technical or mental — and their various scales — local, national, regional or transnational. It is precisely this concrete historicity of the modes of technological implementation that has been ignored by the millenarian discourse of cyberspace, which has shown no interest in the way the functions and uses of the new intelligent tools are socially constructed (Lévy, 1997, 2000). In his time, André Leroi-Gourhan sensed the pitfalls of a certain type of civilisational thinking when he indicated his disagreement with the vision of Teilhard de Chardin, which bore the 'sign of every apocalypse': 'Humanity may very well have to wait for the "omega point" for thousands of years, and in the meantime, as in the year 1000, it will have to organise itself, while waiting, and go on living' (Leroi-Gourhan, 1964: II, 267).

4 Post-industrial Scenarios

Technical forecasting or futurology laid the foundations for ideas designed to announce, if not explain, that humanity was on the threshold of a new information age, and hence, of a new universalism. These ideas sprang from three different sources in succession: the social sciences, forecasting expertise and geopolitics.

The sociological debate

From 'end-of' discourse to post-industrial society

During the 1960s, the 'end of ideology' thesis provided a rallying point for numerous political scientists and sociologists, mainly in the US. It was even given international recognition at a meeting of the Congress for Cultural Freedom held in Milan in September 1955 on the topic of 'The Future of Freedom'. This organisation was founded in Berlin in 1950, and, apparently unknown to the meeting's Italian organisers, was financed by the Central Intelligence Agency (CIA) under the cover of a private foundation. There was nothing unusual about this practice.

At the height of the struggle against 'international communism threatening the "free world"', the vast domain of culture indeed became a strategic component of United States foreign policy. The US government provided itself with both overt and covert means of disseminating the values of capitalism in the world, a fact revealed two decades later by the investigations of the US Senate Committee on foreign and military intelligence operations, headed by Senator Frank Church. Acting under the broad authority granted them by the National Security Act of 1947 and the Central Intelligence Act of 1949, CIA-funded foundations served as conduits of funds for a variety of purposes, including clandestine activities and operational use of the academic community and cultural organisations which supported United States foreign policy (United States Senate, 1976).

A hundred and fifty-six political and intellectual figures gathered together at the conference to discuss the notion of 'free society', including English socialists Hugh Gaitskell and Richard Crossman; Arthur Schlesinger Jr., the future adviser of President J.F. Kennedy; the economist Friedrich A. von Hayek, founder after the Second World War of the Mont-Pèlerin Society and head of an international network of radical free-marketeers who repeatedly attacked Keynesian and Marxist views, insisting that the individual entrepreneur was the measure of all things; the French political scientist Raymond Aron, who had just published *The Opium of the Intellectuals*; and the American sociologists Daniel Bell, Seymour Martin Lipset and Edward Shils. The agenda for debate centred on 'end-of' discourse: the end of the age of ideology, the end of politics, the end of social classes and class struggle, as well as the end of protest by intellectuals and of political commitment. Lipset and Shils went so far as to postulate that sociological analysis was sweeping away ideological prejudice, testifying to the new legitimacy of the 'Western liberal intellectual' (Shils, 1955; Lipset, 1960). Bell was appointed director of the international seminar programme of the Congress for Cultural Freedom.

Another recurrent thesis, first expressed in 1940 by the American philosopher James Burnham, who had broken with the Trotskyist Fourth International, stirred up much discussion of 'ends' or 'twilights' at the time. According to this argument, the managerial revolution and the irresistible rise of 'organisation men' were ushering in a new society – the management society – prefiguring the convergence of capitalist and communist regimes. A community of thought emerged. Daniel Bell commented twenty years later: 'A number of sociologists – Aron, Shils, Lipset and myself – thus came to view the 1950s as characterized by an "end of ideology"' (Bell, 1976: 41).

Mass society and the end of ideologies

The construction of 'end-of' discourse was inextricably linked to the debate over the future of 'mass society'. The essence of mass society and of 'massification' was a nagging question. It had haunted Alexis de Tocqueville when he questioned the danger of uniformity in the 'democratic age'. It contributed to the birth of the social sciences, via the discussion about dissolving 'communities'. In the period between the wars, it included controversies over the crisis of European (high) culture. During the 1940s and 1950s, the notion of mass society was at the heart of the Frankfurt School's critique of the standardisation of the 'cultural industry' as well as the analysis of the 'lonely crowd' carried out by David Riesman and his research team. Backed by the rediscovery of the theme of alienation, in its Marxian and Weberian forms, the theme of massification formed a dividing line between critical intellectuals and 'integrated' ones. On one side were those who denied the emancipatory potential of mass society and mass culture; on the other side were those who ignored questions about the role of mass culture in the system of social regulation, believing instead in the democratising virtues of mass society and culture and their ability to foster greater participation on the part of the masses and reduce the distance separating the centre from the periphery of modern society.

These antecedents explain why Daniel Bell felt he was justified in making the following observation: 'The theory of mass society is probably the most influential social theory in the Western world' (Bell, 1960: 212). They also explain why his colleague, Edward Shils, went even further, asserting that sociology was haunted by the 'spectre of mass society' which sidestepped any discussion about the nature of the 'industrial society' that it presupposed (Shils, 1960). In the second issue of the French journal *Communications*, Bell explained why he considered the term ambivalent: 'One of the favourite landmark expressions of our time is "mass society", which is used to express both the passive aspect of existence and its mechanisation or the disappearance of any criteria of judgment. These various uses of the word reflect reactionary or progressive philosophies, for the expression, which appears to be purely descriptive, is actually loaded with a whole set of judgments about modern society' (Bell, 1963: 1). The journal itself was a party to the controversy, since it had just been founded by Roland Barthes, Edgar Morin and Georges Friedmann and was the mouthpiece of the CECMAS (Centre for the Study of Mass Communications), which the three of them had recently established at the Ecole pratique des hautes études.

Daniel Bell nonetheless challenged such 'judgments about modern society', and more specifically, those made by 'progressive philosophies', in his book *The End of Ideology*, which came out in 1960. In this all-out attack on the denigrators of mass culture, whom he reproached for reducing the terms of the discussion to all or nothing, he postulated that it was impossible to characterise contemporary industrial democracies without invoking the phenomenon of the 'end of ideology'.

In 1960, Daniel Bell published *The End of Ideology*. Thirteen years later, he brought out *The Coming of the Post-Industrial Society*, in which he linked his earlier thesis about the end of ideology to the concept of 'post-industrial society'. This system, he believed, would be free from any ideology: 'The starting point for me was a theme implicit in my book *The End of Ideology* – the role of technical decision-making in society. Technical decision-making, in fact, can be viewed as the diametric opposite of ideology: the one calculating and instrumental, the other emotional and expressive' (Bell, 1973: 34). Bell was engaging here in forecasting, as the subtitle *A Venture in Social Forecasting* indicates. Extrapolating from observable structural trends in the United States, he built an ideal type of society and predicted it would undergo five fundamental mutations: a change in the main economic component (from a production economy to a service economy); a change in the structure of employment (pre-eminence of the professional and technical class); the new core role played by theoretical knowledge as a source of innovation and in formulating public policy; the need to stake out the future by anticipating it; the rapid rise of a new 'intellectual technology' oriented towards decision-making. Bell took the idea of the disappearance of labour in the post-industrial economy so far as to assert that since codified knowledge would henceforth shape the dynamic of innovation, the new society would no longer be characterised by a labour theory of value but by a knowledge theory of value. Bell played Max Weber's theory of bureaucracy against Marx's theory of class struggle. In choosing the descriptive term 'post-industrial', Bell kept his distance from other terms in circulation, particularly the notion of 'post-capitalist society' forged by Ralf Dahrendorf in 1959. In Bell's view, the reference to a 'post-industrial' period was better suited to suggesting, on the one hand, that we live in an 'interstitial time', when new social forms have not yet clearly emerged, and on the other hand, that the sources of this upheaval are, first and foremost, 'scientific and technological'. Bell did not adopt the expression 'information society' until the end of the 1970s. The biomorphic belief in information as the generator of society as a whole was by then already solidly established: 'Every society is an information society and every organization an information organization, just as every organism is an information organism. Information is necessary to organize and to run everything from a cell to General Motors or the Pentagon' (Oettinger, 1980: 192).

The new, decisive aspect of post-industrial society, for Bell, was the expansion of 'human services' (health care, education and social services) and, above all, the development of 'technical and professional services' (research, evaluation, data processing and systems analysis). On average, the class of professionals and technicians was growing twice as fast as the rest of the workforce, and that of scientists and engineers three times as fast. A new intelligentsia was coming into being, with its niche in the 'universities, research organisations, professions and government'. From the standpoint of stratification and also of power, the dominant figure in industrial society was the businessman, while the company was the focal point of social life. In post-industrial society, the central role belonged to scientists, universities and research centres. Since occupation determined class, this social category of specialists linked to new intellectual technology codified and tested theoretical knowledge, the 'axial principle' of post-industrial society. The abstract systems of symbols it developed shed light on the most varied fields of experience and sealed the fate of empiricism. Whereas pre-industrial society had been a 'game against nature', and industrial society a game against 'fabricated nature', post-industrial society was a 'game between persons'. This was demonstrated, in Bell's view, by the principles of cooperation and reciprocity that reigned in the scientific world, especially in research teams, as opposed to hierarchy and coordination.

Scientists above the fray

The 'scientific community', as Bell saw it, derives its legitimacy from its charismatic nature. It is universal and disinterested, a 'charismatic community' removed from ideology 'in that it has no postulated set of formal beliefs, but it has an ethos which implicitly prescribes rules of conduct. . . . As an imago, it comes closest to the ideal of the Greek polis, a republic of free men and women united in a common quest for truth' (Bell, 1973: 380). The vitality of the ethos enables the scientific community to defend itself against bureaucratisation, political subservience and totalitarianism. Science is a vocation. 'The charismatic aspect of science gives it its "sacred" quality as a way of life for its members. Like Christianity, this charismatic dimension has within it a recurrent utopian and even messianic appeal. It is the tension between those charismatic elements and the realities of large-scale organization that will frame the political realities of science in the post-industrial society' (Bell, 1973: 408). There is a fault line separating this intelligentsia, free from ideology and committed to techno-science, from intellectuals with a literary background 'who have become increasingly apocalyptic, hedonistic and nihilistic' (Bell, 1973: 214).

All the new 'intellectual technologies' – linear programming, simulation, information theory, cybernetics, decision theory, game theory, utility theory – substitute algorithms for intuitive judgements. By helping to define rational action and identifying the means to accomplish it, they make it possible to manage 'organised complexity' (the complexity of large systems and organisations and the complexity of theories involving an increasing number of variables). The same applies to 'disorganised complexity', for probability theory has made great strides in the 'problem of the average man'.

Monitoring social change, and for this purpose, creating mechanisms for anticipating the future, became the password to access the post-industrial age. Thanks to new forecasting techniques, it was possible to reduce the margin of indeterminacy in the economic future. The growth of new technologies could be regulated using technology assessment methods. A bill passed in 1967 mandated the US Congress to set up a Technology Assessment Office. Only through planning and control of technology by means of political regulations was it possible to counteract the market mechanisms, skewed as they were by various private interests, and impose respect for 'common needs'. The latter were the responsibility of the 'public economy' or 'public sector', still known as the 'public household' (as opposed to the 'domestic household'), which formed a 'service sector' distinct from the market economy and household economy. That is what Bell meant when he referred to a question of prime importance to post-industrial society, namely the friction between the economising mode, caught up in functional efficiency and the management of things (and of people, administered as things), and the sociologising mode, which took into account non-economic values, necessarily implying reduced efficiency and production. Faced with this divergence between the 'private costs' of the enterprise and the 'social costs' ('externalities', in the language of economists), the only possible arbiter was the principle of social responsibility.

The roots of the new functional society

What were the main features of the ideal-type of 'post-industrial society'? First, it was rooted in a long history of organisational doctrines leading up to the construction of the paradigm of the functional society, of which the post-industrial age was thought to be the crowning stage. In the pantheon of technocracy, Bell included three people: Saint-Simon, known as the 'father of technocracy', Frederic Winslow Taylor and Robert MacNamara. Moreover, Saint-Simon was one of the authors Bell cited most frequently (no less than twenty times). To illustrate the functionality of society-as-organism in the post-industrial age, Bell even borrowed Saint-Simon's metaphors of the orchestra and the crew of a ship (while Taylor had preferred the metaphor of the athletic team). Clearly, Bell's profession of faith in the 'charismatic community' of positive knowledge was comparable to the French philosopher's 'new Christianity'. Finally, Bell echoed

Saint-Simon's denunciation of the negative spirit embodied by the *littérateurs*.

Secondly, there was the vision of history underlying the notion of 'post-industrial'. As a linear movement, it corresponded to the schema of history-modernity-progress, or, as Fernand Braudel would say, to the conception of history 'in slices'. It was bound by the mathematical theory of information. History became a prisoner of probability theory and the ideology of growth (and exponential growth, to top it off), and was seen as unfolding according to a mechanical model of evolution similar to the one set forth in 1960 by Walt W. Rostow in his 'Non-Communist Manifesto' on the 'stages of economic growth': the traditional stage, the transition, take-off, economic maturity and mass consumption. Progress would come to so-called backward countries through the diffusion of the values of so-called adult countries. Innovation and social change flowed from top to bottom; from the central transmitters and technological elites to administered subjects, from societies that had arrived at the highest stage of modernisation and development to those at lower levels. This path has a name, coined by the sociology of modernisation: it is called 'Westernisation'.

Finally, there was the obliteration of network thinking. The idea of irradiation from the centre towards the periphery was developed at every level in the hierarchy. Bell was above all a firm believer in the mission of the welfare state, which required a centralised structure to carry out the task of planning. Thus, a break occurred with the first generation of post-industrial thought, which had emphasised forms of decentralised organisation (see Chapter 2). As a consequence, there was also a break with the heirs of decentralising thought who were also making themselves heard during the 1960s. One of the first environmental journals to come out in England, in 1970, was called *The*

Ecologist: Journal of Post-Industrial Society. The whole decade was rich in indictments of the productivist ideology of macro-subjects and arguments in favour of a return to gentle technologies and micro-subjects (Illich, 1970; Roszak, 1972; Schumacher, 1973; Dickson, 1974).

Uncertainty about economic growth soon upset the hypotheses of this first schema of the information society. Yet, despite flagrant evidence to the contrary, the scientistic vision succeeded in establishing the idea that organisational doctrine had banished politics. Since society was functional, it was managed according to the principles of scientific management.

Expertise

The forecasting boom

Before adopting the notion of post-industrial society as the central argument of his book, Bell had an opportunity to test it as head of the Commission on the Year 2000, launched by the American Academy of Arts and Sciences in the 1960s. A number of scientists and experts took part in the work of the Commission, which resulted in a five-volume report (Bell, 1968). The document shows just how fashionable forecasting had become. During the second half of the 1960s, scenarios of possible future developments mushroomed as networks of forecasting professionals expanded. In 1966, the World Futures Society was founded in Washington, and in 1968, the Institute for the Future. Conferences were devoted to the subject in Oslo (1967) and Kyoto (1970). Journals were launched carrying titles such as *The Futurist, Futures* and *Technological Forecasting.* France was not to be outdone, for it had its own forecasting movement, which included Gaston Berger, the founder of *Prospectives* (Future Prospects) in 1957, a publication of the Centre for Forecasting Studies, and Bertrand, and Hélène de Jouvenel, who created *Analyse et Prévision* (Analysis and Forecasting) to ensure the dissemination of works on 'pragmatic utopia' undertaken as early as 1960 by an international research network called 'Futuribles'. In 1975, the two journals merged into one, entitled *Futuribles*.

Post-industrial society, programmed society, scientific and technological revolution

In 1967, *Civilisation at the Crossroads*, a work by the Czech sociologist Radovan Richta and his research team at the Academy of Science, was published in Prague in Czech and Slovakian. An English edition was brought out, again in Prague, in October 1968. The book's key concept was the 'scientific and technological revolution', which had already enjoyed a long history in the countries of the communist bloc. However, Richta's use of the concept was not in line with the prevailing doctrine, according to which communism alone could release the power of technological forces that were held in check by capitalism. He asserted that a new type of civilisation was coming into being: 'post-industrial civilisation', 'tertiary sector civilisation' or the 'civilisation of services'. He insisted on the key role played by science, along with technical and professional personnel, and the emerging opposition between 'progressive' and 'conservative' attitudes in the face of this structural change, thereby chipping away at the dogma according to which the working class was central to the construction of socialist society. At least, that was how the censors interpreted Richta's book, whereupon they prohibited its circulation and forced the author to publicly disavow it. The book was translated into French in 1969, and had a far-reaching impact on the debate that raged on the left regarding the future of communism. A summary of the book was also published in London (Richta et al., 1969).

In the same year, the sociologist Alain Touraine published *La Sociétè postindustrielle: naissance d'une sociétè* (Post-industrial Society: The Birth of a Society). Although Touraine used the expression in the title, he found 'programmed society' preferable to 'post-industrial society' as a way of designating the new type of society 'taking shape under our eyes'.

> One might call them 'post-industrial societies' to indicate the distance separating them from the industrial societies that preceded them, and which are still mixed in with them, in both their capitalist and socialist forms. One might call them 'techno-cratic societies' to designate the power that dominates them. One might call them 'programmed societies' if one wishes to define them according to the nature of their mode of production and economic organisation. I find the latter term the most useful, because it indicates most directly the type of work and economic action involved. (Touraine, 1969: 7)

Indeed, only the long introduction, intended to give coherence to the four chapters, taken mainly from articles published between 1959 and 1968, even mentions the term 'post-industrial society'.

What sorts of conflicts occur in a society in which the new forms of social domination go beyond the opposition between capital and labour, and in which struggles against economic exploitation, and therefore the working class, are no longer of central importance, as they used to be in industrial society? A society in which power tends towards more diffuse and less openly authoritarian global control, and which attempts to reduce social conflict by the 'dependent participation' of those who are subject to the machinery of economic and political decision-making? In this 'society of alienation which attracts, manipulates and integrates', how can 'creative protest' against programmed change be expressed? In Touraine's work, the analysis of the changes in the 'social game' and the interaction among the actors shifts the emphasis away from the technological and scientific upheavals, which Bell saw as the source of post-industrial society. In his four chapters, Touraine deals successively with old and new social classes, student movements, the rationalisation of the enterprise and the relations between leisure, work and society. For purposes of comparison with Bell's vision of a post-industrial society, the chapter on student movements is clearly the most suggestive. It was written in the wake of the political and social crisis engendered by the events of May 1968 in France, and presents an image of the university that contrasts sharply with that of his American colleague. The university was no longer the sanctuary of the charismatic community, but rather the cradle of an anti-technocratic social movement. In mobilising against the rigid system of political and administrative decision-making of this decaying institution, students were revealing the nature of social conflict in programmed societies.

Daniel Bell's judgement of Touraine, Richta and other 'European neo-Marxist theoreticians' was particularly aggressive: 'While all these writers have sensed the urgency of the structural changes in the society, they become tediously theological in their debates about the "old" and the "new" working class, for their aim is not to illuminate actual social changes in the society but to "save" the Marxist concept of social change and the Leninist idea of the agency of change' (Bell, 1973: 39–40). The problem is that the American sociologist was shooting at anything that moved on his left, at the risk of peremptorily lumping everyone together. In actual fact, Alain Touraine has always explicitly distinguished his positions from those of Marxism.

The second half of the 1960s was a heyday for think tanks. Forecasting methods, it should be remembered, made a qualitative leap during that period (see Chapter 3). Developing anticipatory scenarios became a market in itself. Professional forecasters offered their services to corporations and governments eager for advice and ready to pay for it. The general public was introduced to the new techno-information age from this angle. One prominent prognosticator was Herman Kahn, formerly of the Rand Corporation and co-founder of the Hudson Institute, who developed a number of nuclear strategy scenarios (he invented the language of the 'laddered escalation' for the Pentagon) and wrote the second volume of the final report of the Commission on the Year 2000. The text, reproduced in his classic work *The Year 2000: A Framework for Speculation on the Next Thirty-Three Years* published in 1967, was written in collaboration with Anthony Wiener and prefaced by Bell himself. Kahn drew a picture of the various types of society at the threshold of the third millennium, with the idea of post-industrial society as a backdrop. Kahn's world was divided into five spheres: pre-industrial, partially industrialised, industrial, advanced industrial or mass consumer and post-industrial. His

grid shows a world made up of twenty-one post-industrial countries: twelve 'visibly post-industrial' ones (the United States,
Canada, Scandinavia, Switzerland, France, West Germany and
the Benelux countries) and nine 'partially post-industrial'
(including the Soviet Union, Czechoslovakia, the United Kingdom, Italy, Israel and Australia). Argentina was placed in the
'advanced industrial' category, on equal footing with Spain and
Venezuela, Greece, Singapore, Hong Kong, Taiwan and North
and South Korea. Chile was placed in the industrial stage,
along with Mexico, South Africa, Cuba, Libya, Peru and
Turkey. Brazil was relegated to the 'partially industrialised'
category, alongside China, India, Pakistan and Egypt. Kahn
also forecast that in post-industrial (and post-scarcity) society,
people would work no more than five to seven hours a day, four
days a week, 39 weeks a year, and would take 13 weeks of vaca-
tion.

Interactive democracy

The most renowned of all the forecasters was the independent
consultant Alvin Toffler, author of the bestsellers *Future Shock*
(1970) and *The Third Wave* (1980), who took upon himself the
task to 'bring futurism to the masses', according to the expression used in *Time* magazine (Krantz, 1996: 42).

Toffler, a former Marxist, was quite clear about the function
of anticipatory scenarios. To avoid the 'traumatism of future
shock', it was necessary to create in citizens a desire for the
future within the framework of a 'new theory of adaptation'.
The mission of the 'strategy of anticipatory democracy' was to
give ordinary citizens, and not just a tiny elite, the chance to
take the future into their own hands (Toffler, 1976). Among his

expectations for the future, Toffler mentioned interactive democracy, the de-massification of the mass media, pluralism, full employment and flexibility. Above all, he foresaw the end of that 'dangerous anachronism', the nation-state, and a new opposition emerging between the Ancients and the Moderns, in place of the rich vs. the poor or capitalism vs. communism. At the time, 'interactive democracy' referred to the plan, proposed by certain think tanks, to cable cities and make them a locus of experimentation in techno-communitarian ideology. Indeed, Nicholas Negroponte, the prophet of the first cyberage, author of *Being Digital* (1995) and shareholder of *Wired*, a magazine for Internet fans, prior to founding the Media Lab at MIT in 1979, had worked on this type of urban future-planning at Rand and the IBM Cambridge Scientific Centre. One writer had even imagined a communitarian society, criss-crossed by 'electronic highways' (Martin, 1978).

Active society and techno-communitarianism

Amitai Etzioni, a specialist in modern organisations and professor at Harvard Business School and Columbia University, introduced the topic of participatory democracy into the sociological debate on the emerging society. He refused the term 'post-industrial' because, in his view, future society would be, above all, 'active' and 'post-modern'. These were the two descriptive terms he used as early as 1968 in his book on 'active society', though he was less explicit about the concept of post-modern society than about active society. For Etzioni, the post-modern period began with the challenge to values inherited from the industrial age arising out of communication and knowledge technologies in the wake of the Second World War. The dilemma facing post-modern society was chiefly a moral one, and it concerned control over the instruments it had created. Post-modern society would usher in an era of 'mass participation' (Etzioni, 1968), which explains the pivotal nature of the concept of 'active society', in sharp contrast to Bell's reticence on the topic of 'participatory democracy' in his analyses of post-industrial society.

Etzioni was an active proponent of communitarianism, a philosophy that he traced back to its roots in Ancient Greece and the Old and New Testament, while acknowledging the influence of Martin Buber's teaching: 'Communities are social webs of people who know one another as persons and have a moral voice' (Etzioni, 1995: ix). The notion of 'social bond' is examined from every angle and designated as the key to constructing this new 'moral voice'. Only a responsive society, comprising interpersonal bonds woven around shared values, can reverse the trend towards 'too many rights, too few responsibilities'. Communitarian solidarities help to restore civic virtues in a society in which the notion of rights has gained precedence over that of individual responsibility. This applies to the family community, the school community, the neighbourhood community, the local, regional and national community, and beyond that, the human community. 'Our communitarian concern may begin with ourselves and our families, but it rises inexorably to the long-imagined community of humankind' (Etzioni, 1995: 266).

Towards the end of the 1960s, the communitarian philosopher inspired a project for a participatory technology system, called Minerva, which he developed with the support of the Ford Foundation. Its objective was to encourage the use of cable television in an effort to help democratise decision-making at the municipal level: 'There is no doubt that Minerva and the relay system, modified in the light of experience, will be an integral part of the social communications structure of the future societies which are now possible, the coming era of mass participation' (Etzioni and Leonard, 1971). He proposed that all cable television companies in urban areas set aside one third of their broadcasting time for non-commercial, community organisations. In 1979, Etzioni was appointed as senior advisor to President Jimmy Carter. His importance lies in the fact that his philosophy was not only to become a source of techno-libertarian thinking, but also permeated numerous social-democratic parties in search of an alternative to the idea of class struggle and socialism, the foremost among them, New Labour in Britain.

The geopolitics of the global age

The advent of the technetronic era

The global age is not ahead of us; we are already in it. John F. Kennedy was the first 'globalist' president, for he thought that 'the whole world was, in a sense, domestic politics'. Thus wrote Zbigniew Brzezinski in *Between Two Ages: America's Role in the Technetronic Era* (1970: 307) at the end of the 1960s. In this book, the geopolitical vision lending legitimacy to the American idea of the information society was made quite explicit. Brzezinski, a specialist in communist-bloc issues at Columbia University, examined the effects on international politics of the dawning of the 'technetronic society' and the 'technetronic era'. The former was 'a society that is shaped culturally, psychologically and economically by the impact of technology and electronics, particularly in the area of computers and communications', and the latter, an era in which political processes have become global in scope. Although Brzezinski objected to the concept of post-industrial society, because it did not express the strategic forces behind the change, his analysis coincided with Daniel Bell's in several respects. In particular, he shared Bell's unshakeable faith in the role of science and the university, the latter being destined to become 'an intensely involved think tank, the source of much sustained political planning and social innovation' (Brzezinski, 1970: 12). The worldwide information network that enabled the pooling of knowledge was leading to the formation of an international professional elite and the birth of a common scientific language, a lingua franca that would be the functional equivalent of Latin. The geopolitician did not find McLuhan's notion of the 'global village' relevant, though he, too, used Teilhard de Chardin's analyses to justify the idea of a 'new universal conception of the world', a 'new planetary consciousness', a 'new worldwide unity' seeking its 'own structure, a consensus and harmony on which it would be based'. Instead of a return to the intimate community of the 'village', Brzezinski thought he was witnessing the formation of a 'global city', that is, 'a nervous, agitated, tense, and fragmented web of interdependent relations', producing anomie, anonymity and political alienation.

Brzezinski's reflections were an extension of 'end-of' discourse: 'Constrained ideologies are replaced by constraining ideas, yet lacking the eschatology that characterised other historical times' (Brzezinski, 1970: 114). The dominant passion, he predicted, would be for equality. The pillars of 'ideological universalism' – religion, nationalism and Marxism – were fading from the intellectual horizon. The last great all-encompassing faith – communism – was being split into factions. It had not achieved its original objective: 'linking humanism to internationalism' (ibid.: 193). The fundamental problems facing human beings were those of survival; it was therefore natural to see ideological concerns give way to ecological concerns.

Network diplomacy

The project of universalism was henceforth to be led by the United States. Rome had exported law, England, parliamentary democracy and France, culture and republican nationalism. Now it was the turn of the United States to be the centre from which flowed techno-scientific innovation and mass culture, the product of a model of high consumption. The United States offered the world not only a model for action designed for businessmen and scientific circles, but also, quite simply, a way of life. Confrontation with novelty was, indeed, part of everyday life in America. Its universalism could be explained by the fact that US society 'communicated' more than any other in the world. It was the main propagator of the technetronic revolution, the proof being that it had gone farther than anyone else in building a 'world information grid' through satellite systems. As a result of this ongoing effort, by about 1975, 'For the first time in history the cumulative knowledge of mankind will be made accessible on a global scale – and it will be almost instantaneously available in response to demand. . . . Given developments in modern communications, it is only a matter of time before students at Columbia University and, say, the University of Teheran will be watching the same lecturer simultaneously' (Brzezinski, 1970: 31–2).

The new technetronic hand being dealt out implied a redefi-
nition of the nature of the relationship between the United
States and the rest of the world. Terms such as 'imperialism'
and *pax americana* could no longer account for these new 'complex, intimate and porous' relationships and an 'influence' that
was 'almost invisible'. The economic and cultural borders of
US society were increasingly difficult to pinpoint. The United
States had become the 'first global society in history', prefiguring 'global society' on a worldwide scale. The techno-scientific
revolution 'made in the USA' captivated the imagination of the
entire world, as the conquest of space amply demonstrated.
Inevitably, less advanced countries aligned themselves with
the centre of innovation and sought to imitate it by borrowing
its techniques, methods and organisational practices.

Interdependence made it necessary to grasp the world as an
interconnected unity. Sheer force had become obsolete in the
face of the complex problems of contemporary societies. 'Network diplomacy' had replaced 'gunboat diplomacy'. From the
diagnosis of the state of international relations to the test of
technical change, Brzezinski inferred the necessity of 'global
political planning'. He put forth two proposals in this regard:
first, to restructure the US State Department and create the
position of 'Under-Secretary for Global Affairs'; secondly, to
develop a plan for international cooperation that broke with
the doctrine of the 'Atlantic Community', in other words, to
set up a 'community of developed countries' (Brzezinski,
1974). Such global governance of world affairs would be more
realistic than a 'world government', and would make it possible to focus on disseminating scientific and technological
knowledge. Brzezinski was to be appointed National Security
Adviser under President Jimmy Carter (1976–80). He had to
wait until the Clinton administration to see his wish for the

creation of a position of Under-Secretary for Global Affairs finally fulfilled.

Post-modern society

In 1979, Jean-François Lyotard (1924–98) elevated the term 'post-modern society' to the status of a philosophical concept in *La Condition postmoderne*. The book, originally intended for the Council of Universities of Quebec, became one of the standard texts defining the term. Unlike Bell, who was completely caught up in his belief in techno-science, Lyotard adopted a working hypothesis that knowledge (and the institutions that produce it) changes its status when a society enters the post-industrial age and culture enters the so-called post-modern age. He saw this change as having begun, in Europe at least, towards the end of the 1950s, when post-war reconstruction was completed. The 'post-modern condition' of knowledge meant that the 'grand narratives' that gave knowledge its legitimacy were called into question. Late twentieth century disbelief stemmed from the disintegration of these accounts of the rise of knowledge and the emancipation of humanity, as a result of German idealism and the French Revolution. The crisis of these narratives, which the modern era had invented to represent itself and provide ideological justification for social cohesion, merged with the crisis of the philosophy of history-as-progress. There were no more macro-subjects entrusted with a mission to redeem the world. Vanguards and heroes were a thing of the past, not only in art, but also in politics and in the field of knowledge. The task of legitimising contemporary knowledge excluded any recourse to the Hegelian realisation of mind or Marxian classless society as a criterion of the validity of post-modern scientific discourse.

Lyotard treated scientific knowledge as a 'variety of discourse', based on the fact that the sciences and advanced technologies had taken language as their object for the past forty years. Indeed, computer science and data-processing machines placed before us the 'great language issue', namely, 'something that was missing from the problem of the social bond, justice and the future of developed societies' (Lyotard, 1979: 4). The hegemony of computer science imposes a certain logic; it implies a set of prescriptions determining which statements qualify as 'knowledge'. The two questions raised by Plato are still relevant: Who knows? Who is able? Or again: What is knowing? What is being able? In an age in which the main challenge of knowledge is how to transform it into merchandise and how to incorporate it into new industrial, commercial, military and political strategies, it was aberrant to think that performance or measurable efficiency, in terms of the relation between input and output, could be a criterion of knowledge.

Lyotard's position ran counter to the thesis of the German philosopher Jürgen Habermas, who maintained that in a society guided by an ideology of technology and science, the criterion for the validation of knowledge can only lie in the principle of consensus: the players must agree on the rules of the game and consensus is reached through dialogue between individuals as intelligent, knowing beings with free will. For Lyotard, legitimacy is achieved by dis-sensus: an information system will be legitimised only if it gives rise to the invention of new 'moves' in already existing games, or to new games. What needs to be done is to determine which criteria of judgement and legitimacy have 'local' value. For artists, scientists and logicians, what is at stake is the ability to say or do something different. This is what Lyotard calls the *paralogy* of inventors, in contrast to the homology of experts. The operational language of decision-makers and capitalists is indeed diametrically opposed to the liberation made possible by the multiplicity of language games.

Post-modern knowledge is ambivalent. It is both a new instrument of power and an opening up to differences. The collapse of modern discourse in its claim to unity, universalisation and totality is in itself a guarantee of tolerance and of plurality of cultural expressions.

Zbigniew Brzezinski's postulate about the advent of 'network diplomacy' marked a turning point, and in the 1970s there was talk of a thaw in international relations, a decline in coercive strategies and the emergence of varied forms of interaction. The vocabulary of 'complex interdependence' came into widespread use, and the notion of 'world society' made a noticeable comeback. Strategists paid close attention to the multiplication of poles and flows, whether commercial, financial, migratory, cultural or religious, as well as to the constellation of non-governmental actors that joined together in networks (Keohane and Nye, 1972; Muskat, 1973; Burton, 1976). The traditional system of international relations was disrupted my multinational firms and the non-governmental organisations mobilised to combat the damage resulting from the expansion of the former (Mattelart, 1976, 1996).

Just when Brzezinski was imagining the architecture of the world as governed by scientific reason channelling technological innovation, the new actors in the world economy were undermining the traditional foundations of geopolitics in the name of mercantile advantage. The discourse of the largest multinational corporations concerning 'One World' was based on the rise of information industries and networks, presented as freeing production managers, consumers and products from constraints of national boundaries and connecting them in a single self-regulating market, in order to declare the nation-state irrational, and consequently, the need for public regulatory policies obsolete. This was the guiding principle of the management theoretician Peter F. Drucker when he combined 'knowledge society' and the 'Global Shopping Centre' (Drucker, 1969). By the end of the 1960s, the semantics of globalisation had taken hold among US specialists in international relations and in the circles of corporate 'world leaders'. The lexicon of 'globalness' would continue weaving its planetary web and combining with references to 'information'.

5 The Metamorphoses of Public Policy

Is the nation-state still a relevant framework for thinking about technological development? Many large industrial countries tried to answer that question during the 1970s by domesticating the notion of 'information society', making such language part of the common currency of political thought, and formulating a strategy for reaching the 'new era'. During those years, the principle of regulation seemed beyond question. In the following decade, when the dominant trend had changed to deregulation and privatisation, a similar question was raised, but this time at the level of supranational governance. Negotiations between the United States and the European Union regarding the deregulation of audiovisual and telecommunications systems came to the fore.

The politico-administrative model

The Japanese 'Computeropolis'

From the beginning of the 1970s, the strategy formulated by Japan to meet the challenge of new technologies became a focal point for the large industrial countries. In 1971, the Japan Computer Usage Development Institute (Jacudi) adopted the plan to become an 'information society' as its 'national objective for the year 2000'. The epicentre of this pro-active policy was the MITI, the 'super-ministry' of international trade and industry, whose primary mission was to foster synergies between research and industry, and between the public sector and major private firms. The contours of a future society emerged from this plan. There would be a state-run central databank, distance-controlled medical systems, rationally managed programmed instruction capable of developing a 'computer-oriented state of mind', a system to prevent and combat pollution, an information system for small and medium-sized businesses and a centre for workforce retraining. The backdrop for all this was the Computeropolis model, a city fully cabled, equipped with home terminals, automatic traffic flow management, a network of computer-controlled trains and two-seated vehicles, virtually unstaffed hypermarkets featuring payment by magnetic cards, and computerised air conditioning.

A tower would stand in the centre of Tokyo, where the databanks and centres of scientific research and documentation would converge and all the national 'reservoirs of thought', public or private, would be stored. This 'central reservoir of thought' would not only fuel teaching and research, but also guarantee a new system of grassroots participation thanks to free access to information. An information-processing 'peace battalion' was envisaged to channel the mobilisation of the public towards technological innovation. A chronological table sketched out the four phases of recent Japanese history, starting in 1945 and leading up to the transformation of Japan into the first information society in history. The phases overlapped: the first period (1945–70) was marked by the predominance of mega-science and the 'country' as subject; the second (1955–80) was that of 'organisation' and 'the enterprise'; the third (1970–90) was dominated by 'social services' and 'society'; and the last (1980–2000) by 'private individuals' and the 'human being'. The government and private firms launched experimental social projects such as the Highly Interactive Optical Visual System Information (Hi-Ovis) in residential areas in the suburbs and on the outskirts of Tokyo, to test the attitudes of the participating households (most of them with a housewife) in dealing with these interactive technologies.

The notion of the vulnerability of information systems also appeared. It was stipulated that data-processing services should not fall under the domination of foreign capital, as this would jeopardise economic independence. The extent of foreign interest in a Japanese firm should be less than half.

Japan's infatuation with the information society was apparent in the discourse that accompanied it. The writings of the futurologist Yoneji Masuda promised a society in which intellectual creativity would supplant the desire for material consumption induced by the society of abundance; in which an ethic of self-discipline would accompany social involvement; and in which human beings would live in harmony with nature, while centralised power and hierarchy would give way to a 'multi-centred society' (Masuda, 1980). Yet in the Hi-Ovis projects, women were the main target for the study of possible uses of new technology, whereas the team in charge of monitoring and assessing the experiment was made up exclusively of men (Cronberg and Sangregorio, 1981) – a paradoxical situation, to say the least, for a project that included 'restoring subjectivity' as one of its social aims.

The most obvious result of the early MITI strategy was the breakthrough achieved by Japanese firms in the field of digital memory. They launched the personal computer in 1978, and within four years, succeeded in reversing the trend that gave US companies almost full control over the domestic market. They also consolidated Japan's worldwide leadership in consumer electronics. This period, during which institutions were devised to provide a framework for the information society, coincided, moreover, with accelerated internationalisation and delocalised production by the major companies in this sector. It also revealed Japan's attachment to educational aims, resulting in the fact that by the year 2000 it could pride itself on being the only country in the world to have created educational television channels watched by the general public.

Policies of national independence

The Japanese government's approach was diametrically opposed to the thinking in Canada, whose industrial potential was, of course, not comparable to the economic power of Japan. In 1969 Ottawa appointed a 'telecommission', which produced a final report of 250 pages, published in 1971, under the title of *Un Univers sans distance/Instant World*, based on the opinions and diagnoses of a wide variety of organisations and individuals that were recorded in an 8,000-page preliminary report. The following year, another report came out, more explicitly devoted to the world of information processing, entitled *Branching Out*. This seminal document presented at length a philosophy of decentralised democracy as the basis for a policy of national network appropriation: 'communications must be from the people, by the people and for the people'. The installation of community cable television and experiments with videotext (the

Telidon project) were accompanied by invocations of the 'right to communicate'. However, the government's hopes for founding a national industry on this technology did not last long (Raboy, 1990; Sénécal, 1995; Lacroix and Tremblay, 1997).

During the 1970s, policies of national independence flourished in all parts of the world. India learned its lesson from the abrupt departure of IBM, which had refused to cede a portion of its capital to Indian partners in 1978. Without altering the spirit of Nehru's industrial policy of self-reliance based on planning and massive investment in the public sector, the Indian government encouraged foreign companies to enter into partnerships involving transfers of technology. The government's strategy revolved around an ambitious space programme that was to propel India to the rank of a major power in the field.

In Brazil, as early as 1972, the military government envisioned developing its own computer industry in the name of national security and defence of its national identity. Four years later, a decision was made to set up a Brazilian microcomputer industry, banking on the know-how of university research professors and the transfer of technology from Japanese firms. This policy of national independence, supplemented by the nationalisation of the telecommunications industry, also had a military side (in 1981, weapons industry exports rose to $2.4 billion) (Mattelart and Schmucler, 1983).

In Chile, the Englishman Stafford Beer, a specialist in entrepreneurial organisation and author of *The Brain of the Firm* (1972), made a proposal to the government of the socialist President Salvador Allende (November 1970– September 1973) to put cybernetic engineering at the

service of overall production planning for nationalised enter-
prises. A debate arose within Allende's governing coalition,
Chilean Popular Unity, concerning a possible drift towards
technocracy. Many Chilean theoreticians in the cognitive
sciences acquired their initial training in this programme to
develop synergies, known as Cybersyn. When General
Pinochet seized power on 11 September 1973, the original,
if controversial, experiment came to an abrupt end (Beer,
1975; De Cindio and De Michelis, 1980).

The Nora–Minc report: a philosophy of crisis

Outside Japan, a country largely spared by economic recession,
the idea of 'crisis' infiltrated the discourse of the large industrial
countries regarding computerisation strategies. Paradoxically,
the very notion of 'crisis' had rarely been examined in depth
(Schiller, 1984), until the report by Simon Nora and Alain Minc
on the computerisation of society, submitted to French President Giscard d'Estaing in January 1978. This document was
one of the few that went beyond paying mere lip-service to the
notion. It echoed the worrying diagnosis of the state of the world
that had been circulating since the beginning of the decade.
First, there was the Club of Rome report on the 'limits of
growth', published on the eve of the first 'oil crisis' by a group
of economists, ecologists and specialists in political science and
international relations, who explained that the Western model of
growth was self-consuming; it devoured people, raw materials
and natural resources, and was hence bound to exhaust itself
(Meadows et al., 1972). Then there was the report on the 'governability' of Western democracies, drafted by three specialists in

the social sciences at the request of the Trilateral Commission, a sort of private advisory staff for the leading industrial countries. This report warned of the 'potentially desirable limits to indefinite extension of political democracy' (Crozier et al., 1975). By the time the Nora–Minc report was drafted, the threat of an energy shortage had already made the spectre of economic crisis look familiar.

Simon Nora and Alain Minc carried out an in-depth study of the notion of 'economic crisis' in order to achieve an overview of the problem and propose a solution to it, in keeping with Saint-Simon's doctrine on crisis and the role of reorganisation assigned to the network. 'The increasing computerisation of society,' they wrote, 'is at the core of the crisis. It can either aggravate the problem or help solve it'. It has created an upheaval in the 'nervous system of organisations and society as a whole'. The 'new global method of regulating society' which, in their view, should be introduced, would be able to curb the decline in social consensus and regenerate agreement at the grassroots level with the rules of the social game: 'This reflection on information processing and society has strengthened our belief that the equilibrium of modern civilisation rests on a delicate alchemy: finding the proper balance between the increasingly vigorous exercise of the sovereign powers of the state (even though they need to be better channelled) and the growing exuberance of civil society. For better or for worse, information processing is going to be part of the equation' (Nora and Minc, 1978: 51). The authors dressed their ideas in redemptive discourse: because *la télématique* (a French neologism invented for the occasion to signify the combination of telecommunications and computerisation) promised more flexibility in managing consensus, it would open the way to 're-creating an information agora'. In the long run, the network society would call into question 'the elitist distribution of power, which ultimately means knowledge and memory'. On the other hand, it would be a 'random society', Nora and Minc explained, that is, the 'locus of an infinity of decentred conflicts'. The values of the information society are the focal point for competing forces and the outcome is still uncertain. These values require 'feedback on the desires of autonomous groups towards the centre, and infinite expansion of lateral communications'.

The process of externalising collective memory, accelerated by digitalisation, must cope with the risk of monopolisation by foreign databanks or, as Nora and Minc warned: 'Knowledge will end up being modelled on the stock of available information.' Building up one's own databanks will become 'indispensable for sovereignty'. The source of the challenge was clearly designated: IBM had just announced its intention to enter into the field of satellite communications (Nora and Minc, 1978: 131). The 'spirit of public service' must guide the response to this challenge. Only action taken by the public authorities to standardise networks, launch satellites and create databanks can 'allow leeway to develop an original model of society' and a 'new model of growth'. The policy was to be spearheaded by a large French Communications Ministry in charge of the post office, telephone and telegraph department (PTT) as well as the space programme and multimedia activities.

In 1978, a law on computer data and freedom was adopted by the French Parliament and an *ad hoc* Commission (the CNIL), was given the task of enforcing it. The law was the result of a stormy national debate on the dangers of computerisation, following the revelation of a project, developed in 1973 by the French Ministry of the Interior, for an automated system of administrative records and directory of individuals, known as

Safari, based on the cross-referencing of 400 different files using a single ID code, the Social Security number (Vitalis, 1981, 1998). In late 1978, the government appointed a commission to study how cross-border data flows affected the protection of personal data in the context of increasing competition between economies in post-industrial society. For the author of the report, certain worrying trends were appearing on the horizon. The main risk was the scenario of a 'terminal-based society', which, for the weakest countries, would mean a society reduced to the dimensions of a market, fuelled by imported products, due to delocalisation facilitated by networks; states would be reduced to accommodating on their territory 'only scattered fragments of business activities managed at the supranational level', (Madec, 1980). This early political effort to take border-crossing networks into account was to result in a specifically French doctrine regarding such flows. Unlike the United Kingdom, Belgium or the Scandinavian countries, France continued to oppose the principle of the free flow of data brandished by the US authorities (Palmer and Tunstall, 1990). In the wake of the presidential election of May 1981, the Socialist government inaugurated an industrial strategy 'wagering on scientific research and technological progress as driving forces to bring the country out of its economic crisis'; the strategy sought to 'democratise computerisation' rather than 'computerise society'. The rhetoric invoked social demand rather than technological supply. Four years later, deregulation and the demands of international competition brought back a more pragmatic discourse on modernisation through computerisation (Jouët, 1987). None of this prevented US experts on information highways from taking an interest in the Nora–Minc report, translated by the MIT press and prefaced by Daniel Bell, or from monitoring the adventure of the Minitel, one of the few projects for an interactive system undertaken in a large industrial country and intended for the general public prior to the rise of the Internet (Bell, 1999: xxii).

Towards a neo-liberal model of competition

The United States and diminishing state control

The proliferation of anticipatory scenarios in the United States did not hasten the decision on a policy for entering the information society. Yet the federal government took up the issue of telecommunications and began circulating the term 'information society' almost at the same time as Japan. A further indication of its importance was the fact that American universities were the first to develop a field of study directed towards computer-assisted decision-making: Communications Policy Research. These studies reflected a bias in favour of reduced regulations. Regulation itself was considered to be the consequence of the ideological debate, dating back to the nineteenth century, on the distinction between private property and social property (Sola Pool, 1974).

In 1970, President Richard Nixon transformed the structure of governmental decision-making in the field of cable, computer and satellite technologies, with the founding of the Office of Telecommunications Policy (OTP), a coordinating body reporting directly to the White House and headed by an expert from the Rand Corporation. With the 1969 moon landing, the United States had reached the end of the technological innovation phase of the conquest of space. The watchword was now the application of electronics to 'social needs'. In 1971 this idea inspired the project for a system of national networks, formulated by NASA and various US educational institutions at the request of the President's personal advisors in a report entitled *Communication for Social Needs: Technological Opportunities* (National Aeronautics and Space Administration, 1971). 'It is becoming increasingly clear in the United States,' the introduction states, 'that there is a set of national problems that could be resolved through telecommunications'. The list of priority areas included education, public health, the enforcement of law and criminal justice, postal services and a warning system in the event of a political emergency or a disaster. The welfare state was in its heyday at the time. It was logical, therefore, that the report should emphasise unequal educational opportunity, especially when it affected the children of ethnic minorities. The aim of the new distance education system was quite simply 'to develop attitudes favouring the development of flexible citizens who, as many people have already realised, are the kind of citizen the twenty-first century is going to need'. Future expectations were along the same lines: 'By the year 2000, the separation between home and school will to a large extent have vanished'; 'school buildings will no longer be anything but centres for the distribution of electronic educational programmes, community centres and sports centres, practical laboratories and places for artistic experimentation' (Mattelart, 1976). At the same time, the large telecommunications firms were predicting that distance work would be the lot of three-quarters of the active population.

The debate on the proper strategy for building the information society would be settled only after a pragmatic, tortuous process extending over several decades. In 1969, the Democratic President Lyndon B. Johnson had set the judicial machinery in motion to combat monopolistic practices at IBM (the firm controlled three-quarters of the US computer market). In 1974,

Nixon's successor, Gerald Ford, in turn undertook antitrust proceedings against another giant, this time in telecommunications: American Telephone and Telegraph (AT&T). The Carter administration (1977–80) abolished the Office of Telecommunications Policy and replaced it with an agency, the National Telecommunications and Information Administration (NTIA), which was placed under the authority of the Department of Commerce. The reason for this shift lay in the emerging mode of regulation for the whole communication system. Indeed, the new Communication Act proposed to revise completely the rules of the game defined by the establishment of the Federal Communications Commission (FCC) in 1934. The idea was to put an end to the 'natural' monopoly of AT&T and thereby undermine the philosophy that gave it legitimacy, namely that the preservation of the public interest required a single network under the control of a public regulating body. The measure, which reduced the scope of control exercised by the regulatory telecommunications administration, reflected another decision, also made during the Carter presidency, in favour of the gradual withdrawal of public authorities from the field of civil aviation and ground transport.

Rulings were made on the antitrust suits against the telecommunications and computer giants in January 1982, under the Reagan presidency. AT&T was allowed to keep its laboratories and continued to handle long-distance calls and supply telephone equipment to customers, but it was required to dispose of its twenty-three local telephone companies. The suit against IBM was finally dismissed. The new Republican administration abruptly abandoned thirteen years of legal proceedings and took on the defence of the multinational company, which had been accused of abusing its dominant position by the European Community (65 per cent of the mainframe computer population).

In 1984, Brussels cleared IBM of any suspicion of misconduct in exchange for minor concessions.

The deregulation of the entire communications system in the United States under President Ronald Reagan took place at the same time as the Defense Department was making a spectacular return to technological innovation through the Strategic Defense Initiative (SDI), known as 'Star Wars'. The project, launched on 23 March 1983, was aimed at building an anti-missile system based on satellites, capable of stopping enemy salvoes in mid-air. The plan for a global electronic missile shield, which had more to do with science fiction than anything else, came to nothing. It was placed on the back burner, only to be revived by President George W. Bush in 2001. On the other hand, the bonanza of investment injected new dynamism into the military applications of artificial intelligence. In the wake of SDI came the Strategic Computing Initiative, a vital complement (Mosco, 1989). The Japanese had just announced their project for a fifth-generation computer. The Americans retaliated by placing the Defense Advanced Research Projects Agency (DARPA) in a unifying role, akin to that of Japan's own super-ministry of industry. The command, control, communication and information systems developed by the agency would be tested during the Gulf War of 1991.

The debate over the free flow of information

The 1970s can be considered the high point of the international debate over the neoliberal doctrine of the free flow of information, defended by the US State Department (see Chapter 3).

The advent of the movement of non-aligned countries gave the debate a dimension it had lacked when confrontations within international organisations were basically limited to opposition between the United States and the Soviet Union. The discussions that took place at UNESCO were concerned with achieving a new balance in the flow of information, which moved disproportionately from North to South. The states of the South insisted on the need to usher in a 'New World Information and Communication Order' (NWICO). Although this demand provided many of them with an easy way to clear themselves of any responsibility for the lack of transparency and freedom of the press in the third world, it nevertheless raised a real and widespread problem. The report of the Commission for the Study of Communication Problems, set up by UNESCO and chaired by Sean McBride, the Irish Nobel prizewinner and co-founder of Amnesty International, finally put a match to the powder keg (McBride, 1980). The United States under Ronald Reagan and the United Kingdom under Margaret Thatcher seized the pretext of an increasingly 'politicised' debate to walk out of the international organisation in 1985 and 1986, respectively, soon followed by Singapore. Their actions ignored Marc Porat's warning in his official report on the information economy: 'The question is wholly political, not technical' (Porat, 1978: 78).

Clearly, the widespread protest against the imbalance in information flows and US State Department doctrine had the effect of accelerating thinking within the political establishment itself regarding the geostrategic stakes of the information society. In 1977, the US Senate Foreign Relations Committee held its first hearings on the 'information age'. The Committee, presided over by Senator George

McGovern, listened to testimony from media managers, corporation heads, academics, trade union leaders and even a former director of the CIA. The hearings endorsed the definition of information as a 'new national resource'. The Committee's report, published under the title *The New World Information Order*, emphasised three issues that were to remain on the agenda: 'How can the flow of information be increased to better all mankind without impinging upon personal privacy, proprietary data, and national security? How can – or should – the Second and Third Worlds' desire to rigidly control information sectors of their societies be accommodated, while trying to allow the free flow of information worldwide? How can the US Government organize to protect our security, cultural and economic interests and also help meet the needs – and gain the cooperation – of the developing nations?' (Kroloff and Cohen, 1977).

The spread of the notion of the information society

References to the 'information society' began to compel recognition in international organisations. In 1975, the Organisation for Economic Development and Cooperation (OECD), whose membership consisted of the world's twenty-four richest countries, used the notion for the first time and hastened to call upon the expertise not only of Marc Porat, but of other US specialists as well. One of them, Ithiel de Sola Pool, was the recognised leader in research on communication deregulation policy. Four years later, the Council of Ministers of the European Community also adopted the notion and made it the key word of a five-year experimental programme (FAST – Forecasting and Assessment in the Field of Science and Technology), which was set up in 1980 (Bjorn-Andersen et al., 1982). The United Nations Centre on Transnational Corporations examined imbalances in transborder data. The thesis of development 'without reserve or constraint', defended by Washington, was hardly in favour at the time (Becker, 1987). The International Labour Organisation and the major trade unions expressed their concern about the possible repercussions of computerisation for employment (Jacobson, 1979; Rada, 1981).

In 1980, after four years of work, the Council of Europe adopted the 'Guidelines governing the protection of privacy and trans-border flows of personal data'. The agreement was binding. Its crucial innovation was to specify in its first article that anyone, 'regardless of nationality or place of residence', could take advantage of the stipulated guarantees and rights. That same year, the OECD adopted a recommendation concerning 'cross-border flows of personal data', with a similar intent, except that it was only a recommendation and member countries were not bound by it. Both documents called upon governments not to issue regulations that would go against the free circulation of registered information, on the pretext of protecting privacy. Twenty years later, the obvious ambiguity of this phrase was to rekindle the dispute between Europe and the United States, when the European Union directive on the protection of personal data came into force in October 1998. The US authorities and 'global marketers' viewed the directive as an impediment to building databanks and perfecting 'target' tracking and profiling methods, both of which were indispensable tools of electronic commerce.

In 1979, two events, with very different aims, suggested the complex issues involved in introducing new technologies: the

World Administration Radio Conference (WARC) and the OECD Interfuture project. The first one brought up for renewed discussion the issue of redistributing radio frequencies (monopolised since the beginning of the century by the major sea powers). The conference, which was organised by the International Telecommunication Union, heralded the shift of the debate on future society towards organisations with technical competence at the expense of institutions with a cultural vocation such as UNESCO (Smythe, 1980). The second event involved the study of the 'future evolution of advanced industrial societies in harmony with that of developing countries' in view of the 'decisive qualitative leap' represented by microelectronics. The project's subtitle says a lot about the uncertainties that paved the way to the information society: 'Facing the Future: Mastering the Probable and Managing the Unpredictable' (OECD, 1979).

In 1977, IBM orchestrated its first advertising campaign around the advent of the 'information age': 'Information: there's growing agreement that it's the name of the age we live in.'

Deregulation

Global operators

The years 1984–85 marked a turning point. First of all, the deregulation of financial markets, which opened up the world to the free flow of capital, provided a clear picture of the networks of the global economy, but also revealed the risk of economic crisis in the absence of supranational regulatory mechanisms. On the other hand, the divestiture of AT&T, which took effect on 1 January 1984, set off a worldwide shock wave, which hastened the deregulation of telecommunications against a backdrop of technological change (digitalisation, high-speed networks, optoelectronics, increased memory capacity and lower costs). In Europe, the neoliberal government in Great Britain took the initiative to privatise British Telecom in 1984. Public telecommunications companies, forced to comply with the rule of free competition, gradually moved towards a status that allowed them to operate across their borders. The process became irreversible in January 1998, when the agreement on the opening of competitive markets came into effect. This had been concluded a year earlier by sixty-eight governments, following three years of negotiations within the framework of the World Trade Organisation (WTO), the successor to the GATT. Aside from the fact that some signatory countries (such as Brazil, Canada and Japan, for example) reserved the right to set a ceiling on the investment of foreign firms in national telecommunications systems, more than half of the 135 members in the trade organisation had not yet signed on by the year 2000. Unlike the International Telecommunication Union, which is one of the specialised bodies of the United Nations system in which each member country has a vote, the countries in the WTO are free to sign or not sign agreements concocted mainly by the countries of the triad (the US, Europe and Japan) whose interests are over-represented.

The shift to competitive status had repercussions for the entire communications system. The struggle was on to become one of the rare global operators capable of offering telecommunications services (telephone, data transmission, etc.) via a so-called seamless network. The scope of their activities continued to widen, with merger-acquisitions and cross-investments generating increased overlap between content providers and network operators. The stakes of these operations rose, leading to greater concentration of capital, improved technologies and merger operations in the stock market that took place at such a pace it would be tedious to try and list them all (McChesney, 1997). The high point of the wedding of 'new economy' networks to those of the 'real economy' came in January 2000, with the takeover of TimeWarner, the world's leading multimedia group, by AOL, the world leader in Internet access. AOL's ambitions were clearly stated on the walls of its headquarters: 'AOL everywhere, for everyone'. This meant nothing less than being present throughout the entire chain, from content production to distribution, in every medium currently existing and yet to come! A few months later, and in response, another mega-merger took place, starting with a takeover bid by the French multimedia 'champion' Vivendi-Universal-Canal-Plus. These mega-mergers illustrate the irrational exuberance of the Internet bubble and the increasingly influential role of finance in this sector of economic activity. The strategic mistakes of some corporations, and the spectacular bankruptcies of others, offer a glimpse of their opaque accounting operations.

The promise of information highways

In 1987, the Green Paper on telecommunications initiated a process of consultation among member states of the European Union with a view to defining the terms of public policy. The document recommended the abolition of national monopolies and raised the question of using information networks as a potential basis for the construction of a single market. During the next decade, no fewer than three directives were to map out the path towards deregulation, unrestricted competition and universal service.

In 1993 the United States launched the National Information Infrastructure programme. The European Union immediately followed suit. The White Paper on growth, competition and employment, submitted in late 1993 by Jacques Delors, presented a framework for reflecting on Europe's response to the US project for building information highways. This programmatic document enumerated the 'challenges' and traced out 'pathways' for 'entering the 21st century', but also expressed major concern about the problem of unemployment. Reports on the information society and information highways drawn up by official bodies in various countries, such as the Théry report in France, or the Information Society Initiative in the United Kingdom or the Info 2000 report in Germany, revealed that Europe was still far from speaking with a single voice. When the time came to formulate a strategy for establishing information routes, these national specificities became an issue, since they referred to specific configurations of actors in different institutional, cultural, industrial and political contexts (Vedel, 1996).

In March 1994 the US information highway project became a springboard for a worldwide strategy, with Al Gore's proposal to build a Global Information Infrastructure (GII). It was no accident that he decided to make his announcement in Buenos Aires, the capital of a country that had chosen a neoliberal path, before an audience of delegates to the plenary meeting of the International Telecommunication Union, in which the main topic was 'telecommunications and development'. Gore struck a prophetic tone in his keynote address: 'The Global Information Infrastructure offers instant communication to the great human family . . . I see a new Athenian Age of democracy forged in the fora the GII will create' (Gore, 1994). The avowed objective of this vast crusade was to abolish the world's great social imbalances. The prerequisite for obtaining the rewards of new technologies was to deregulate national telecommunication systems. The Democratic Vice-President was ill-inspired to mention the case of Mexico as an example of the flamboyant success of neoliberal open-market policies, for just a few months after the meeting in Buenos Aires, the World Bank's most brilliant pupil of structural adjustment policies plunged into an unprecedented financial crisis that put the country on the verge of social collapse, whilst deep in the state of Chiapas, Mexico, the neo-Zapatista movement gave birth to a new mode of resistance to the neoliberal order by appropriating the network of networks for its own purposes. It was in the same year – 1994 – that the notion of the 'new economy' began to appear in official discourse.

The US project for a National Information Infrastructure

During the US presidential campaign in 1992, Bill Clinton's running mate, Al Gore, introduced the topic of information highways, thereby rallying to the Democratic cause the traditionally Republican manufacturers of Silicon Valley. The previous year, Robert Reich had laid the economic and political foundations for what was to become the National Information Infrastructure project. Reich, an economist and future Secretary of Labor during President Clinton's first term, demonstrated that there was no limit to the sale of 'symbol manipulation services' in a global economy and that the United States was in the best position to meet the challenge of information engineering by gaining the edge on its competitors. (Reich, 1991). The plan could succeed, however, only by overcoming the shortage of 'Symbolic analysts'.

As soon as Clinton arrived in the White House, he set up an Advisory Council on the National Information Infrastructure.

The project promised to create large numbers of well-paid jobs for highly qualified people, to reform the educational system, ensure universal access to health care and inspire the reinvention of democracy. Nevertheless, the gap between the discourse on technical remedies and the reality of social policy soon began to widen. The objective of health care was abandoned when plans for reform were defeated in Congress. This outcome generated fear that the use of telediagnostics and telemedicine techniques would only reinforce segregated access to health care. As for the educational system, the government gave up trying to curb its rampant crisis. The end result was a delay in updating training programmes, which would have been consistent with the idea of a far-reaching technological project to increase prosperity and growth by diversifying skills. The aborted project prompted Robert Reich to observe: 'It is partly due to the budget deficit, but this is not only the federal government's doing. State and local governments are also less interested in making the required investments. The states spend more money on building and maintaining prisons, for example, than on higher education' (Reich, 1997: 69). The promise of participatory democracy was reduced essentially to communication policy gimmicks such as making certain sites, starting with the White House, available to 'interactive citizens', and keeping them up to date on official policies. The project, in short, was stripped of its social attractions; only the economic aspects remained. The information highway now became a 'historic turning point for our trade', and 'essential to America's competitiveness and economic power', in the words of President Clinton.

The Bangemann Report on *Europe and the Global Society of Information*, published in May 1994, presented itself as an adaptation to the new reality. Prepared by a group of experts from the telecommunication and media industry, the document recommended rapid deregulation of telecommunications, arguing that it would bring productivity gains, favour technological innovations and encourage cultural pluralism. 'When products are more easily accessible to consumers,' stated the authors, 'the possible vehicles for conveying cultural and linguistic diversity that abound in Europe will be further increased.' They expressed concern about the brakes on free circulation (and therefore freedom of expression) inherent in obstacles to competition, such as policies of restricting cultural products, through quotas or by invoking intellectual property rights. The spirit of the report was in sharp contrast to Jacques Delors' White Paper a few months earlier, in which he emphasised the importance of the state and public policies.

In late February 1995, the Brussels meeting of the G7, composed of the world's wealthiest countries, officially ratified the concept of a global society of information and simultaneously reiterated the members' solemn determination to deregulate telecommunication markets as soon as possible. The G7 summit was the first to be devoted to that subject. Al Gore made a speech on the 'Promise of a New World Order of Information'. It was the consensus of the gathering that the building of information highways should be left to private sector initiative and the virtues of the market. Some fifty managing directors of major European, American and Japanese electronics and aerospace firms took part in this historic meeting, but no representatives of civil society were invited to attend. This did not prevent the participants, in the concluding statements, from invoking the ideal of 'human enrichment'.

In July 1997, President Clinton outlined Washington's position concerning electronic commerce: governments must respect the original nature of this medium and allow global competition and consumer choice to define the rules of the game for the digital market. In December of the same year, a new Bangemann report came out on the convergence of telecommunications, the media and information technologies. The author of this Green Paper adopted an interrogative tone in presenting a choice of three options (adapt existing regulations, adopt a minimal regulatory regime for new services only or rethink the regulations completely). Clearly, the interrogative tone was deliberately used to soften the argument that accentuated even further the distinctly liberal proposals of the previous report on the global information society: technological convergence calls into question the principles justifying the application of different regulations to different industrial sectors or member states; the 'global environment' is not suited to excessive or inappropriate regulation; the challenge to regulations based on scarcity from an information society based on abundance cannot be dissociated from the challenge of globalisation. In short, having too many rules is not compatible with geo-economic necessity. However, the debate on the report did not lead the European Union to choose the 'minimum regulation option'. A consensus was reached in favour of adapting existing regulations.

In March 2000, at the European economic and social summit meeting in Lisbon, the European Union adopted the strategic objective of becoming 'the most competitive and dynamic knowledge-based economy'. The role of educational systems was defined evasively; they were called upon to 'adapt to the needs of a knowledge-based society as well as to the need to raise the level of employment and improve its quality'. There was still no mention of content and uses, unless one considers that the mention of the need for teachers to become Internet users qualifies as a 'policy'. Just as the European Social Charter made only limited prescriptions, there was no consensus on Europe's criteria for educational quality. Educational policy, like social policy, continues to fall within the province of individual member states. Subordination to short-term economic policy, punctuated by a series of deadlines (deregulation of capital markets in 1990, the single market in 1991, the single currency in 2002) was structurally written into the European 'Constitution'. The only European political power in the strict sense of the term is the Central Bank. Hence, the vacuum created by the absence of a clear long-term policy (Fitoussi et al., 2000).

Cultural industries and convergence

With the opening of the eighth round of multilateral trade negotiation under the auspices of the GATT (General Agreements on Tariffs and Trade) in 1986, the issue of cultural exchange was no longer confined to Europe, as it had been under EU policies on the harmonisation of advertising and television systems. During this new series of talks, known as the Uruguay Round, culture and communication became officially integrated into GATT nomenclature under the heading of 'services', and were treated as such. The official recognition of this technical body as a locus for political prescription in the field of communication became clear on the occasion of negotiations between the United States and the European Union regarding the application of free-trade policy to cultural industries. This test of strength ended in Brussels in December 1993 with the adoption of the so-called 'cultural exception' thesis, an expression that would be abandoned six years later, because it was too strongly associated with the French position, and replaced by 'cultural diversity'. In any case, culture was not to be governed by free-trade rules. A consensus was reached *in extremis* among members of the European Union, though some questioned not only the effectiveness but even the very principle of such measures. Furthermore, within the countries in favour of making culture an exception to the rule, such as France, which led the revolt, the government's position collided with the strategies of major multimedia groups or national 'champions', which were eager to reach the critical mass required to succeed in the world market and therefore opposed to any form of protectionism, out of fear of retaliation. The fact remains that the US delegation failed in its efforts to outlaw national subsidies for television film and programme production and distribution, or to defeat the measures taken by the European Union in 1989 following the directive on cross-border television. The US State Department learned from its failure and adjusted its position, attempting to get around the obstacle by keeping the debate on the image industries tied to the issue of current technological transformations. State Department officials saw to it that restrictive measures concerning such cultural products were not extended to new communication services (Mattelart, 1996). They also backed the thesis that digital convergence required cinema and television regulatory systems to merge with those applied to telecommunications and that both should be subject to simplified standards dictated by 'market forces'. Every possible forum was used to discuss the generic question of deregulation of investment in order to counter the thesis in favour of public regulation in the cultural field. One example was the negotiations that took place between 1995 and 1998 within the OECD, bringing together the twenty-nine richest countries in the world to discuss the Multilateral Investment Agreement (MIA). By proposing to free private international investment from restrictions of any kind imposed by the national policies of host countries, the agreement sought to nullify any form of regulation that gave preference to European cultural investments.

Without seeking to reduce the question of the regulation of cultural exchanges to a technical equation, one cannot fail to recognise that the growing interpenetration of communication media has tended to decompartmentalise the debate. One proof is the controversy over intellectual property rights, the primary source of wealth in the information society, on which the very definitions of the notions of 'creation' and 'author' depend. Until now, intellectual property questions in Europe have been governed by the notion of *droits d'auteur* (author's rights), which was defined internationally by the Berne Convention in 1886, according to which authors retain sole control over their work, with royalties paid to them or their heirs until seventy years after their death. As the Internet and other on-line services expand, there is a danger that this will give way, in the name of total deregulation of information flows, to a strictly economic notion of copyright whereby authors sell their rights to producers, who then have a free hand to adulterate the work or use it for other purposes. By recognising intellectual property as an inalienable right through the protection of the author's moral rights over the work, the European Union ratified the former conception in 1996 in a Green Paper on '*Droits d'auteurs* and similar intellectual property rights in the information society' and a directive

issued the following year. There remains the complex problem of setting up an institutional system to protect authors'
rights to ownership of and control over their works, and to
allow them a say in how they are disseminated.

In order to establish a framework of common values, the partners would have to share, at the very least, roughly the same
conception of the responsibilities of public authorities. It is
clear, however, that the 'neoliberalism with a human face' of
market-driven society, as promoted by New Labour in Great
Britain and its 'Third Way', has little to do with the idea of
public policy. Once the norm of individual self-regulation has
been proclaimed, the educational system can no longer be
viewed as a structure that generates social inequalities which
need to be overcome, and instead becomes a place where flexible
individuals construct their own 'employability' within the logic
of school competition, and in which the individual becomes
solely responsible for his or her possible unemployment. This
type of social-liberal pragmatism prevailed at the European
summit in Lisbon in March 2000, where London, Berlin and
Madrid led a dominant coalition in promoting a strictly instrumental vision of the mission of the educational system and of
teachers in the transition to a 'knowledge society'.

There was, however, widespread insistence on the need to
'stimulate actively the acquisition of knowledge and skills' in
order to 'transform the emerging information society into
a knowledge society'. Indeed, in a report specially requested
by the European Commission from a 'high-level group of
experts' from outside the institution, one can read: 'We wish to
emphasise the absence of social integration in the European
debate on the information society and criticise the technological

determinism at the core of the experts' political discourse. The European information society of the future raises a number of social challenges. These challenges transcend the simplistic idea of a rapid adjustment to a future determined by the "outside" pressure for technological change over which individuals have no control' (European Commission, 1997). Given the danger of reinforcing the head start of some regions over others, notes this independent report, an intra-European process for learning and catching up will have to be implemented.

6 The Geopolitical Stakes of the Global Information Society

The techno-informational paradigm has become pivotal in the geopolitical project designed to ensure the geo-economic reorganisation of the planet around the values of market democracy in a unipolar world. The planetary horizon conditions the forms and manifestations of protest against the worldwide order now being prepared.

War and peace in a unipolar world

A revolution in diplomatic affairs

Revolutionary language has emigrated to the neoliberal camp, which turned the notion of 'information revolution' into a sort of Russian-doll term with totalising pretensions: revolution in diplomatic affairs, revolution in military affairs and managerial revolution. Let us examine the image of world order to which each of these expressions refers, starting with the 'revolution in diplomatic affairs'.

Some three decades after Zbigniew Brzezinski's analysis of the advent of the technetronic age, the concept of 'network diplomacy' is reconfiguring the parameters of hegemony: 'Knowledge, more than ever before, is power,' assert the political analysts Joseph S. Nye and Admiral A. Owens, White House advisors. 'The one country that can best lead the information revolution will be more powerful than any other. America has apparent strength in military power and economic production. Yet its more subtle comparative advantage is its ability to collect, process, act upon, and disseminate information. . . . The information edge is important as a force multiplier of American diplomacy, including 'soft power' – the attraction of American diplomacy and free markets' (Nye and Owens, 1996: 20). The sources of this new power include free information (the type of information created by marketing, television and the media, propaganda without any 'financial compensation'); commercial information, which has a price tag and is at the heart of electronic commerce; and strategic information, which is as old as espionage (Keohane and Nye, 1998). The information system, and above all the World Wide Web, is becoming the vector of 'the enlargement of a peaceful community of democracies, which is ultimately the best guarantee of a secure, free, and prosperous world' (ibid.: 36). Soft power is the ability to arouse in others the desire for whatever it is you want them to desire, and the faculty of leading them to accept the norms and institutions that produce the desired behaviour. It is the ability to attain objectives through attraction rather than coercion. As Nye explains, 'Soft power can rest on the appeal of one's ideas or the ability to set the agenda in ways that shape the preference of others. If a state can make its power legitimate in the perception of others and establish international institutions that encourage them to channel or limit their activities, it may not need to expend as many of its costly traditional economic or military resources' (Nye, 1990).

Strategists, for their part, have advanced another notion: Netwar. This term applies to the new forms of low-intensity conflict pursued by non-governmental players who circumvent governmental hierarchies through networks and demand that the latter retaliate by the same means. Under the heading of 'non-governmental actors', strategists include both so-called activist or participatory movements, such as NGOs, and guerrilla movements, terrorists and drug cartels! One strategy in particular caught the early attention of the specialists: that developed by the neo-Zapatista movement since December 1994, the date of its first information campaign. Relayed across the Internet by a network of non-governmental organisations in Mexico, the United States and Canada that had been mobilised in the past against the North American Free Trade Agreement (NAFTA), this initial action succeeded in bringing international pressure to bear against the offensive planned by the Mexican army to liquidate the guerrilla forces in Chiapas. US army journals and military advisors have since turned this experience into a textbook case (Swett, 1995). At the request of the Pentagon, the Rand Corporation even drew up a report entitled *The Zapatista Social Netwar in Mexico* (Arquilla and Ronfeldt, 1998). Spurred by the diagnosis of network vulnerability in the face of attacks by terrorist groups or organised computer hackers ('hacktivists'), the lessons of this case were even formalised into a doctrine. The fear of an 'electronic Pearl Harbor' has given rise to a number of FBI and Pentagon initiatives intended to organise the defence of the 'nervous system of the nation'. The FBI, for example, is now equipped with a centre for the protection of the national infrastructure. The US Army has created new 'information war' units to intervene in international computer networks. Netwar and cyberwar are the two components of the war of knowledge or 'noopolitics', a neologism derived explicitly from the notion of 'noosphere' developed by Father Teilhard de Chardin (Arquilla and Ronfeldt, 1999). The term 'cyberwar' applies to wide-scale military conflicts whose forms have been modified as a result of intelligence technologies.

Revolution in military affairs: information dominance

During the Dayton peace talks in 1995, a three-dimensional virtual map of Bosnia, produced by a PowerScene field display system, was projected onto a large television screen in the negotiating room and succeeded in bringing the presidents of Bosnia, Croatia and Serbia to agree on the lines for a cease-fire. A lesser-known fact is that, during the same sessions, PowerScene simulation software was also used to demonstrate to the parties involved in the conflict how NATO planes would be able to strike their targets with remarkable accuracy, should the negotiations fail (Anselmo, 1995). These new information tools bring to the fore one dimension of the 'Revolution in Military Affairs' on which Pentagon strategists pride themselves, by turning the experience in Bosnia into a classic case of 'virtual crisis management'.

The conflicts in former Yugoslavia and, before them, the Gulf War – all wars in which NATO turned into a quasi-autonomous security organisation, deciding on military operations by itself – precipitated the geostrategic transformation (Owens, 2001). US supremacy in the field of information technologies was confirmed in the field with systems known in military jargon by the acronym C4ISR: Command, Control, Communication, Computation, Intelligence, Surveillance, Reconnaissance. Information dominance, a spin-off of the Strategic Computing Initiative in the Reagan era, shaped the discourse on the ideal and abstract notion of a perfect, clean war, a war of 'surgical strikes' and 'collateral damage'.

The notion of 'US national interest' has been updated to take into account the United States' new position of 'lonely superpower', in Samuel Huntington's words, or head of the 'system of systems' (Huntington, 1999). There can no longer be any question of intervening in the wars of 'failed states', that is, states considered irretrievably bogged down in tribal conflict or other types of war belonging to the pre-information age. Those types of war are causing the implosion of Africa, for example, where state structures are decomposing and are, in any event, incapable of fulfilling the geo-economic tasks assigned to them by the new global order (Joxe, 1996). So-called 'moral wars', undertaken in the name of universal human rights, can therefore be waged only in certain areas. Despite the information available to the Western powers, in the spring of 1994 they allowed Hutu extremists to massacre nearly a million Tutsi civilians in the space of a hundred days.

The new doctrine is adapted to the fundamental logic of economic globalisation. The accelerated construction of the planet as a system requires thinking in terms of an offensive strategy of peaceful enlargement of the market throughout the world. The days of the defensive strategy of containment in a bipolar theatre of operations are over. The new strategy for global security gives priority to extending the universalising model of 'free-market democracy', for which the control of networks is vital (Gompert, 1998). Mobilising the market is all the more justifiable, the strategists claim, in that more than 95 per cent of Pentagon communications now travel through civilian channels.

The new approach to war was popularised in a bestseller: *War and Anti-War*, by Alvin and Heidi Toffler. Written after the Gulf War, the book provided a particularly revealing key to understanding the doctrinal change, since defence strategists have adopted the authors' vocabulary (Toffler A. and H., 1993). The book examines the convergence of the civilian and military spheres. The cliché of history moving in waves is used to develop a hierarchy of wars, based on whether they belong to the first wave (agrarian), the second wave (industrial) or the third wave (civilisational). The 'civilisational wave' establishes the pre-eminence of 'intangible resources', an all-purpose category in which the authors put ideas, innovation, values, imagination, symbols and images.

However, the experts on the 'revolution in military affairs', obsessed by the experience of sanitised victories against Baghdad and Belgrade, were mistaken in their forecasts. Faced with retaliation against the death squad of 11 September 2001, the doctrine of 'war with zero casualties' (in their own ranks, of course), promoted since the Gulf War, suddenly appeared outdated. The US military machine realised that it had not made its 'revolution' in the face of a 'new battlefield' where so-called asymmetric conflicts now pitted them against opponents who take the initiative and do not play by the rules of the game.

Introspection was not on the agenda. In the Manichaean context of a crusade against the Jihad, the beating of the war drums against the forces of 'evil' drowned out the voices of those throughout the world who, while expressing their compassion for the victims of the attacks, also demanded that the root causes of the world's disorder be finally addressed. The wretched of the earth who feel humiliated and consider that they, too, have a right to remember, did not hesitate to recall the ravages, past and present, provoked by a 'lonely superpower' which, for the first time in history, is in a position to impose its point of view on the entire world.

A global intelligence system for a global economy

A strategy of enlargement presides over the adaptation of the system of global remote surveillance by satellite to the needs of commercial warfare. Thus, the Echelon network, set up in total secrecy in 1948 by the United States and its four affiliates (Canada, Great Britain, Australia and New Zealand) to gather a maximum amount of military information on the Soviet Union and its allies, has been converted into an economic intelligence system. This system of unfettered eavesdropping run by the National Security Agency (NSA), attached to the Pentagon, intercepts, with complete impunity, the telephone calls, faxes and e-mails of foreign companies, using Intelsat civilian satellites for transmission. Some non-governmental organisations such as Greenpeace are also targeted by the system.

Three signs indicate the importance attached to global information dominance. In 1996, the Pentagon set up a new agency alongside the NSA called the National Imagery and Mapping Agency. One of its objectives is to control and centralise the commercial use of the flow of outer space imagery throughout the world. In May 2000, the United States eliminated the selective scrambling of their Global Positioning System (GPS). Launched for military purposes in the 1970s under the supervision of DARPA, this system for localisation at any point on the planet was made available for civilian uses during the following decade, but with reduced accuracy. One of the factors behind this change of orientation was to prepare for possible competition with the European Galileo project to construct a worldwide system of terrestrial detection.

Finally, in 2001, the United States launched a massive spy satellite programme under the responsibility of the National Reconnaissance Office (NRO), which is in charge of planning satellite espionage for the Air Force, working in tandem with the NSA. In 2001, the NRO was operating six spy satellites on an ongoing basis, three Keyhole satellites for optical and infrared observation in fair or overcast weather and three Lacrosse satellites for radar reconnaissance in bad weather and at night. The new project, known as Future Imagery Architecture, consists of preparing by 2005 to run a set of twenty-four spy satellites weighing only a third as much as the earlier ones and capable of collecting 8 to 20 times more images within a margin of accuracy of 15 centimetres. According to experts, it is the most expensive programme in the history of the 'intelligence community'.

Bogged down in technological determinism, the inordinate faith of national security agencies in the omniscience of intelligence obtained via the sophisticated systems of spy satellites and worldwide eavesdropping was exposed as an illusion by its failure to detect the preparation of the apocalyptic attacks of 11 September 2001. On the one hand, the all-technology approach at the expense of human intelligence (or *Humint* as it is called in espionage circles), proved hopelessly inadequate when confronted by faceless enemies, agents of a new global terrorism. On the other hand, the macro-system was incapable of seeing through the 'steganography' techniques used to camouflage Internet messages by hiding them in apparently insignificant images, texts and photographs.

The September attacks resulted in the creation of a new Office of Cybernetic Security, responsible for protecting the country's electronic infrastructures, under the authority of the Office of Homeland Security. A bill known as the 'USA Patriot' Act was passed (the name being an acronym for the mission it was intended to fulfil: Uniting and Strengthening America by Providing the Appropriate Tools Required to Intercept and Obstruct Terrorism). The focus on security has also led to reinforcement of the electronic surveillance of US citizens, via wire-tapping and computer searches.

The project for a global panopticon is similar to the project for a panopticon of everyday life. At least, that is the conclusion one might draw from an article by an intelligence officer in *Military Review*, the official journal of the US Army. The article comments on the substantial progress achieved in the field of software that has enabled marketing specialists to develop detailed virtual mapping of consumers, their characteristics, purchasing trends and other data concerning their actions and the flow of goods (for example, MapLinx and Lotus Domingo). It concludes by stating: 'Just as Bill Gates adapts these concepts to the life of the consumer, soldiers and diplomats should begin exploring their application to conflict-prevention mechanisms. . . . The concept termed *virtual peacemaking* (VPM) is in need of further elaboration, especially since the military and consumer sectors are converging, implying one can assist the other in helping to prevent conflict' (Thomas, 1999: 56).

The manifesto for a frictionless capitalism

A world without mediators

Apologetic discourse on the information society has veered between two diametrically opposed axioms: that we are entering a new era of mediation, and that we are exiting from that same era. The contradiction implied in this double discourse is only apparent, for the arguments converge in testifying to the fact that key social and economic factors have been evicted from the models built for introducing digital technologies and their networks. The tendency to expurgate the notion of power itself is omnipresent. The first axiom presupposes that virtually infinite mediations now involve such a wide range of actors and the worldwide techno-system has reached such a degree of complexity that no one is in charge any longer, and hence, no one is accountable. This is the discourse of theoreticians of global management, for whom the world is not only 'borderless' but also 'leaderless' (Ohmae, 1985, 1995). The second axiom postulates that intermediaries are coming to an end in every field. Bill Gates, convinced that he has invented a 'frictionless capitalism', keeps repeating in his books that sellers are directly communicating more information on their products and services to buyers, and that, in exchange, the latter provide more information on their tastes and buying practices. E-commerce is thus seen as circumventing intermediaries and restoring the natural fluidity of exchange. This rather peculiar two-way form of quid pro quo obviously eludes the question of more and more refined techniques for tracking 'customer capital' and generating loyalty, that is, the increasing Taylorisation of the field of consumption.

As for Nicholas Negroponte, he has continued to hammer home the leitmotif of the end of the nation-state as collective mediation. It is even one of the main clichés in his bestseller *Being Digital*, a collection of some of his columns in *Wired* magazine. He writes that the network, like a neo-Darwinian force that cannot be stopped or even contained, renders the notions of centrality, territoriality and materiality null and void. The four cardinal virtues of the information society – decentralisation, globalisation, harmonisation and empowerment – are poised to bring down the archaic Leviathan. 'In the same ways that hypertext removes the limitations of the printed page,' he writes, 'the post-information age will remove the limitations of geography. Digital living will include less and less dependence upon being in a specific place at a specific time, and the transmission of place itself will start to become possible' (Negroponte, 1995: 165). Whom is Negroponte empowering? The individual as a free-floating unit, sovereign in a free market.

The void left by the fading away of the state is being filled by the return of a communitarian utopia in which references to Jefferson, 1960s California communes and communitarian philosophy are jumbled together (Kapor, 1993). The technolibertarians have made it their catechism. The need to free oneself from an omnipresent state is the core message of the 'Declaration of Cyberspace Independence' proclaimed by the co-founder of the Electronic Frontier Foundation and of the charter of the pioneers of WELL (Whole Earth 'Lectronic Link), set up in California in 1985 (Barlow, 1996; Rheingold, 1993). The 'new electronic frontier' being a founding myth *par excellence*, it is shared by all the independence-seekers of cyberspace. The manifesto 'Cyberspace and the American Dream: A Magna Carta for the Knowledge Age', drafted in 1994 by a collective and distributed by the Progress and Freedom Foundation, repeats almost word for word the argument popularised by Alvin Toffler some twenty years ago. 'The complexity of Third Wave society', he wrote,

is too great for any centrally planned bureaucracy to manage. Demassi-
fication, customization, individuality, freedom — these are the keys to
success for Third Wave civilization. . . . If there is to be an 'industrial
policy for the knowledge age', it would focus on removing barriers to
competition and massively deregulating the fast-growing telecommunications and computing industries. . . . Next, of course, must come the
creation — creation of a new civilization, founded in the eternal truths of
the American Idea. It is time to embrace these challenges, to grasp the
future and pull ourselves forward. If we do so, we will indeed renew
the American Dream and enhance the promise of American life. (Dyson
et al., 1994)

The supposed weightlessness of virtual communities and of
the Net economy provides no protection from reality, however.
The techno-libertarian myth of the end of the nation-state lost
its lustre in the ashes of the twin World Trade Center towers.
With the united front against the enemy, ultra-neoliberal
America rediscovered the virtues of nationalism and government intervention. The digitally empowered citizens also
seemed ready to sacrifice some of their privacy for greater
security.

The industrialisation of training: the death of the intermediary?

A study on industrialisation of training conducted by a group
of researchers from France and Quebec, at the intersection
of communication sciences and education studies, under-
mines the belief in spontaneity secreted by the technological
illusion. It reads in part:

In the face of orders addressed to them both in school and outside,
trainees have neither the means nor the leeway of ordinary cultural
industry consumers. This is due to the fact that they lack, almost by

definition, prior knowledge of what they need to know, and are consequently hardly in a position to find in themselves the means of autonomy when they do encounter these resources, which is a far more constraining situation than it seems. In fact, by a sort of vicious circle, they are expected to have at the outset the very skills they are supposed to acquire by the end of their training. Under such conditions, and in spite of sensational proclamations and promises of a revolution in education using the metaphor (if not the rules) of a market in which service and acquisition would be equivalent to supply and demand, the project of self-service rests on a postulate that is far from self-evident: the ability of users to make themselves autonomous subjects from the outset of the pedagogical process, whereas in all likelihood, their status puts them in the position of having to acquire an autonomy they cannot possess until they have completed their training. The problem of viability is thus posed at the same time as that of the pedagogical value of the industrial transformation at stake. (Moeglin, 1998: 129–30)

This reorganisation of the educational relationship is in keeping with broader social logics, linked in particular to the 'hegemonic tendencies of the seller–customer model and the consumer practices relating to it, as well as to the extension of the ideal of a pay-as-you-go society'. This ideal contradicts the 'principles governing the spheres of production and use of collective, public goods'.

It should be noted that the topic of 'deconstruction of the university', forced to submit to the leitmotif of entrepreneurial flexibility, has become one of the nodal points of critical research on the neo-Fordist ideology of the knowledge society (Webster, 1995; Robins and Webster, 1999). The stakes have become especially crucial as the number of projects for global virtual mega-universities based on this model is on the rise (Mansell and Silverstone, 1996).

A world without partitions

A number of 'ready-to-think' concepts, such as horizontality, fluidity, flexibility, actor autonomy and civic sense have become woven around today's central paradigm of the firm as the owner and master of all criteria of initiative and performance criteria. It, too, draws on a belief in the power of information technologies (still known as 'coordination technologies') to revolutionise social relationships. From the credo of the network firm, with its porous and not always visible boundaries, flow a variety of management values that play on the contrast with the oppressive figure of the closed, compartmentalised, hierarchical mode of Fordist organisation.

The stability of the forms of organisation and management and the permanence of the geographical location of power are fading before the imperative of constant adaptability and the tendency to delocalise everything. Power becomes protean and enters a state of continual metamorphosis.

Integration and omnipresence are the key words. The corollary is the overstepping of boundaries, whether physical or functional. The local, national and global levels overlap harmoniously. Design, production and marketing are conceived as synchronous activities. The container and the content, hardware and software join together. This cluster of closely related notions has given rise to its own newspeak: the verb to 'glocalize', a neologism created by Japanese managers to express the circularity of the local and the global; 'intermestic', invented by American futurologists to indicate the vanishing line of demarcation between international space and domestic space; 'co-producer' or 'prosumer', which establishes the user as a fully-fledged partner in the production process.

The notion of network is the new Proteus. The network enterprise has been accorded the status of symbol of the end of the contradiction between labour and capital, which had handicapped the industrial age. According to the thesis of the sociologist Manuel Castells, the only actors left standing are networkers or knowledge workers, promoted to the status of a new ruling class, because they are the bearers of the 'spirit of informationalism'. Thus, the cyberworld is emptied of its social actors and the work process is viewed simply as a technical relationship. Yet, whether we like it or not, the informational mode of development continues to 'be developed for and put at the service of a set of property relations and the goal of accumulation, not vice-versa' (Garnham, 1998: 109).

Behind the scenes, inside the network enterprise, pressure is put on employees who are tested on management projects, which they are required to complete successfully; those same employees are 'formatted' using methods developed to reveal their personality traits and assess their ability to adapt to requirements. Procedures of industrial organisation impose their quick pace on the labour process and are now extending into the service sector, which is facing keener competition. From keystrokes to videotaping and digital recording of computer operations, workers can be sure that pervasive surveillance of their activities is taking place (Schiller, D., 2000). Assembly-line workers, mostly women, are exploited in the electronics industry in tax-free zones, etc. Outside the enterprise, the management model serves as a standard for the new 'control society', involving short-term control, with quick but ongoing and unlimited turnover, which has replaced the coercive mechanisms of disciplinary societies (Deleuze, 1990; Deleuze and Guattari, 1991). For those who are excluded from the techno-global system, these repressive mechanisms continue to form the horizon of everyday life.

The minimal state

> The 20th century was only a parenthesis of state control. . . . We respond to the question of poverty by saying that the more freely an economy is allowed to operate, the more jobs it creates, the better salaries it pays and the fewer poor people it creates. . . . The intervention of the state is necessary only for the army, the police and the justice system. Everything else can be managed by the private sector. To my mind, the new economy is clearly in tune with this project of freedom. (Boaz, 2000)

This view was expressed by one of the heads of the Cato Institute, a think tank associated with libertarian currents, the most radical in the neoliberal family. Its sole doctrine concerning networks is that they should be governed by commercial law.

In the same vein, the chairman of AT&T did not hesitate to impart the following lessons to governmental delegates assembled at the Telecom 99 conference organised by the International Telecommunication Union in Geneva:

> The global communications revolution can be the first revolution in history that has no losers. . . . The flywheel that drives the communications revolution is moved by the forces of competition and technology. New technology generates new competition. And new competition in turn generates new technology. That's the way it works in any free market. In the communications market, it is industry that has to supply the technology and the competition, while public policy has to create the environment where the flywheel can keep turning smoothly, an environment where new technology and new competition can enter the market without obstruction. . . . But once the environment for competition is created, regulators must have the self-restraint to keep their hands off the flywheel. Thus, the focus of the regulation must change. (Armstrong, 1999)

The Progress and Freedom Foundation, another conservative think tank, was more down-to-earth in its lobbying efforts, proposing in its report *The Telecom Revolution: An American Opportunity* (1995) that the electromagnetic spectrum no longer be considered a 'common good' to be managed by public bodies and instead become private property. The holders of broadcasting licences would thus own their portions of frequencies and would be free to use, develop and sell them as strategy dictated, while the rest of the spectrum would fall within the new realm of 'electronic private property'. Public regulatory bodies would thus become obsolete. The point would be to stimulate more innovative use of frequencies via the invisible hand of supply and demand. This philosophy of self-regulation, which leaves everything to exchange on the market, is reminiscent of the one governing private trading of 'pollution rights' as a way of ensuring environmental protection.

A world without laws

Management reasoning is the 'technical version of politics' (Legendre, 1997). The freedom of citizens to express their opinions is ordered to make way for 'free commercial speech', in other words, to allow the market mentality to penetrate every nook and cranny of the public sphere. Thus, the neo-populist notion of a global democratic marketplace has become naturalised and with it, the clichés about individual freedom of expression and choice – but for individuals in a state of social weightlessness. The definition of cultural diversity is turned into a plurality of service offerings to consumers with free will.

This is the vocabulary used in the Bangemann reports, for example. The arguments put forth by the information industry lobby against the European directive on the protection of individual data are formulated in similar terms: 'Restrictions in the name of protecting privacy must not prevent the right of legitimate business from being exercised by electronic means, inside as well as outside borders' (Eurobit et al., 1995).

The freedom to communicate will brook no prohibition. The reservations that can rightfully be expressed regarding this conception of freedom are immediately rejected by pressure groups as attempts to restore censorship. Only the sanction exercised by consumers on the free market should govern the circulation of culture and information flows. The principle of self-regulation is used to delegitimise any attempt to formulate national and regional public policy in this domain. No room is left to examine the role the state should play in shaping the environment of information and communication systems, in order to preserve the possibility of free expression at the grass-roots level from the logic of segregation inspired by the market and technology. No interest is shown in looking at how the organisations of civil society could be used to exert decisive pressure in demanding such arbitration from public authorities. The whole world is transformed into 'consumption communities'. The word 'community' has clearly never been used in such an indiscriminate and hollow way.

Pockets of resistance

Techno-apartheid

Along with transparency, 'egalitarianism' is another key word in the jargon of techno-utopias. The belief in a new Athenian age of democracy nourishes hope for a way out of the spiral of poverty. The main lesson that history teaches, however, is that in the course of building the world economy, the social forms adopted by networks not only link people together but continue to widen the gap between economies, societies and cultures, divided across the demarcation line of development (Braudel, 1979; Wallerstein, 1983).

The evidence that is starting to accumulate makes it difficult to maintain the lyrical prophecies about the power of reticular tools to overturn hierarchies and push back the logic of segregation. In 1999, the United Nations Development Programme report confirmed that most countries were being increasingly pushed to the sidelines as regards computerisation, while within each country, a sharp line – the 'digital divide' – separates the data-rich and the data-poor (UNDP, 1999). 'The typical Net user,' said the report, 'is a male under 35 years of age, with a university degree, a high income, living in a city and speaking English'. Out of the 13,000 villages in the Senegalese countryside, barely 3,000 were equipped with telephone lines and 65 per cent of the population were still illiterate. In South Africa, which was well equipped with computers compared to the rest of the Continent, many hospitals and three-quarters of the schools did not have telephone lines. More simply, one might add that at a time of shimmering promises of information highways, many countries and regions of the world still do not have a national road network worthy of the name and one third of the world's population has no electricity! The OECD countries represent 19 per cent of the world's population, yet they account for 88 per cent of Internet users, about half of whom are found in the United States, which accounts for only 5 per cent of the world's population. It should be pointed out that that, just as in the nineteenth century, when London was the undisputed hub of the transcontinental network of underwater cables, today the United States has become the nodal point through which Net users from less developed countries must go in order to connect with each other.

The situation in India is telling with regard to the complex double standard within the global system of technology. This country is the world's second-ranking exporter of software after the United States and the leading exporter of computer engineers. Yet, with more than one billion inhabitants, in 2001 the country had only 26 million telephone lines and the rate of penetration of the Internet was in the neighbourhood of 0.2 per cent. Two indicators shed light on the brain-drain phenomenon, which further aggravates the problem. One quarter of the computer firms established in Silicon Valley since 1980 are run by Indians or Chinese. In 2000, the United States altered its immigration laws to allow for the entry of computer engineers in demand. The developed countries of the US–Europe–Japan triad alone account for 85 per cent of scientific research, both public and private: Japan and the Asian dragons (18.6 per cent), Western Europe (28 per cent) and North America (37.9 per cent). Equally worrying is the fact that non-industrial countries that have deliberately decided to start a forced march towards the information age are adopting a strategy that is not only elitist but also authoritarian. That is the case, for example, on the small island of Mauritius, which has taken Singapore as a model to escape from its dependence on textile workshops run by delocalised multinational companies. A more extreme example still is that of the People's Republic of China, which hopes to join the first-world countries by creating special economic zones that function like tax-free ghettos inside Chinese territory, and by relying on a pyramidal system of higher education. The universities are rigorously classified in a hierarchy and the 15 per cent of secondary school graduates who are selected to study in them are screened on the basis of their marks. Alongside the strategy to expand commercial and scientific use of the Internet, filters have been set up to block access to sites deemed undesirable, requiring Net users to register with the authorities. China's entry into the WTO, approved in 2001, which is forecast to result, over time, in the opening up of 49 per cent of telecom and 50 per cent of Internet capital, has in no way been accompanied by a real opening up to foreign operators. The deregulation that has occurred within the country has been aimed at strengthening high-performing domestic operators as a way of resisting the shock of competition and making it as balanced as possible, once the borders have been officially opened.

When the potential to computerise society is reached under the economic model of unbridled globalisation, development gaps turn into apartheid. The digital era is accompanied by a redrawing of territories, with fortress-like centres, operating as veritable enclaves, along the lines of new company towns in the United States, and firms in which employees live cut off from the world in planned spaces, cooped up in the midst of video-surveillance systems and linked together by networks, in total opposition to the immense no man's land of the excluded data-poor. Town planners have expressed their fears that this schema will be transposed to the dematerialised city of the future, with a virtual hyper-centre, a 'meta-city', which already exists in embryo in the project for information highways. In short, a city centre that is simultaneously everywhere and nowhere, accessible solely through new technologies and surrounded by large, unwired outlying areas (Sassen, 1994; Virilio, 1996).

Sustainable development and cyberspace

In the year 2000, UNESCO organised several regional workshops on the ethical, legal and societal changes of cyberspace in Africa, Asia and the Pacific, Latin America and the Caribbean and Europe/North America. In 2001, a year dedicated officially to 'Dialogue among civilisations' on the basis of a proposal by the Iranian President Khatami, the General Conference of UNESCO situated the struggle against the digital divide within the scope of 'INFOethics' and proposed a set of recommendations to the member states 'on the use of multilingualism and universal access to cyberspace', failing which the 'process of economic globalisation would be culturally impoverishing, unfair and unjust' (UNESCO, 2001). The strategy was called the B@bel Initiative. UNESCO also reiterated that basic education and literacy are the 'prerequisites for universal access to cyberspace'. The diagnosis of inequality in the face of new technologies prompted it to organise, together with the International Telecommunication Union, a World Summit on the Information Society (WSIS), to be held in Geneva in December 2003, to discuss the need for 'global regulation'.

After the meeting in Geneva, the next step is to be another summit in Tunis in 2005. UNESCO and the International Telecommunication Union have jointly determined the criteria for ensuring the 'participation of civil society' in the summit process. The primary criterion used in UN organisations to define 'non-governmental organisations', however, sidesteps the issue of grassroots social representation. This category includes not only 'third sector' organisations (in relation to the two other stakeholders, the state and the market), but also trade and corporative organisations such as the International Chamber of Commerce, the Association of Information

Industries, the World Federation of Advertisers and the International Advertising Association. Private-sector interests are therefore being given double representation: first by the organisations created to protect corporate interests and secondly by the leading firms in the computer and telecommunication industries. The strategy of UN agencies is increasingly to encourage these corporations to 'make their voice heard' wherever the fate of the 'global information society' is being debated, and to get them involved in programmes designed to reduce the 'digital divide'. That is one of the reasons why the latter notion is starting to become commonplace, thereby avoiding the question of the social divide.

Alongside these official negotiations, a worldwide, diversified network of non-governmental organisations working in the communications sector, such as the ALAI (*Agencia latinoamericana de información*), the World Association of Community Broadcasters and the World Association for Christian Communication, has seized the occasion of the preparation of the World Summit to launch a far-reaching democratic debate on sustainable development and new information technologies, by organising regional seminars and discussion groups to draft joint positions that will carry weight on the official agenda.

The idea is to consider knowledge and information as 'common, global property' because it is an integral component of the public sphere. This implies a definition of the 'right to communicate' at the grassroots level, as opposed to the mercantile doctrine of the free flow of information (Burch, 1999; O'Siochrú, 1991; Downing, 2000; Raboy, 2001).

The democratic appropriation of new interactive technologies requires patient dialogue between cultures, but in the opinion of numerous experts, this does not always occur in North–South relations (Mansell and Wehn, 1998). Steve Smithson, a professor at the London School of Economics, described the situation this way:

> I recently took part in a colloquium in which a major international telecommunication operator made an edifying speech to the political authorities from developing countries who were in the room. He was incredibly arrogant, saying 'you should do this, you should not do that,' explaining that his products were the best and obviously they should buy them. I had the feeling that colonial days were not far away, and that the markets of developing countries were, above all, a way of making comfortable profits. . . . The role of local public authorities is decisive in reducing the digital divide. (Smithson, 2001)

The opinion of Michael Dertouzos, the director of computer laboratory sciences at the Massachusetts Institute of Technology (MIT) is also of great interest, for it goes against the current of techno-redemptive ideology propagated by his futurologist colleagues: 'I have talked about this with Bill Gates and we profoundly disagree with each other. If the information revolution is left to its own devices, it is going to widen the gulf between the rich countries and the poor countries, and between the rich and poor within each country. History teaches us that if we don't do anything, we cannot exclude violent reactions to this revolution' (Dertouzos, 1999).

There are already lessons to be learned from experiments conducted throughout the world: Kothmale Community Radio in Sri Lanka (1989), the Village Knowledge Centres launched in India in 1998, the Gasaleka & Mamelodi Telecentres (1998) in South Africa, InfoDes (*Información para el desarrollo rural*) in Peru (1998), Nasaseke Multipurpose Community Telecentre in Uganda (1999), Local Radio Network in Indonesia (1999), etc. Many of these experiments attest to the fact that 'the Internet has a better chance to succeed as a tool for development and

participation if linked to existing communication and information experiences. . . . The convergence between radio and
Internet is one of the most interesting symbioses that new technologies can offer. Not only does community radio get empowered to reach new latitudes, but also Internet users learn from a
participatory experience that has done much for social change
during the past fifty years' (Gumucio Dagron, 2001: 30). The first
assessments also reveal material restrictions that limit action.
The Village Knowledge Centres in Chennai, India illustrates the
problems facing development in the poorest areas:

> The vast majority of Web sites are in English, a language that more
> than 95 per cent of Indians do not speak. Nonetheless, the project has,
> since its inception, challenged this by translating and producing local
> contents in Tamil. Poverty itself is a huge limitation. Only 12 public
> telephones and 27 private telephones exist in the project area, which
> covers 19 villages, with a population of 22,000. Routine power failures
> and overloaded telephone lines make connecting to the Internet a frus-
> trating proposition. There are serious questions about whether coun-
> tries like India, weighed down by high rates of illiteracy and illness,
> should spend heavily to provide villages that desperately need schools
> and health clinics, with what most would consider a luxury. (ibid.: 323)

Towards a global civil society?

It was widely thought, prior to the year 2000, that the momen-
tous calendar change would result in widespread computer
bugs. History decided otherwise. In late November/early
December 1999, non-governmental organisations, trade unions
and consumer associations massively mobilised in Seattle, on
US territory itself, to protest against the excesses and dangers
of a '100 per cent market' world, on the occasion of the third

conference of the World Trade Organisation (WTO). The aim of the summit was to start a new round of talks with the goal of arriving at a General Agreement on Trade in Services (GATS) which would extend the law of free trade to sectors that could be rightfully considered 'public goods', such as culture, health, education and the environment. Protesters challenged the very legitimacy of the system of major multilateral financial and trade institutions designed to dominate the process of globalisation, and stigmatised their anti-democratic methods and the over-representation of the wealthy countries. Less spectacular, but just as significant, was the concerted action inaugurated in April 1998 and spread out over three years, whereby more than 600 organisations in some 70 countries used e-mails and web sites successfully to interrupt the MIA (Multilateral Investment Agreement) negotiations launched by OECD with the objective of totally deregulating investments.

The 'Seattle effect' was so strong that henceforth every summit meeting touching on 'global problems' drew protests, including Davos, Washington, Bangkok, Okinawa, etc. The members of the G8 met in July 2000 in the Japanese city in the presence of the bigwigs of the computer world to sign the 'Charter for a global information society', in which they reiterated their determination to defend intellectual property ownership, and combat pirated software programs, continue deregulating telecommunications, promote common standards and protect consumers. An 'operational force' made up of experts, known as Dotforce or Digital Opportunity Taskforce, was even set up to propose solutions to the 'worldwide gap in the field of information and knowledge'. The 'street' did not take long to retaliate. The Jubilee 2000 group burned a laptop computer in front of the conference centre to denounce the hypocrisy of proclaiming a charter filled with good intentions, which proposed to facilitate access to the Internet in poor countries, while remaining evasive about the decline of public development aid, which had fallen to its lowest level in fifty years, and the problem of the debt, which in some countries was absorbing more than half of the annual budget. One ironic detail: Sub-Commander Marcos used the same kind of computer to communicate with the networks of opponents of neoliberalism!

At the Genoa summit in July 2001, the members of the G8 voted to revive the Okinawa project and promoted a 'plan of action for strengthening democracy and the rule of law through e-government'. This generous wish stood in sharp contrast to the extreme violence used by the police to suppress the peaceful demonstrations of the anti-globalisation movement protesting against the increasing interventionism of the rich countries in the management of world affairs. The outline for action proposed by the 'world management board' to stamp out the digital divide was a trial balloon for developing a new form of world governance combining the public and private sectors (corporations and their philanthropic foundations). Indeed, the members of the G8 did not try to hide their intention to work outside the traditional bureaucratic channels of the UN agencies.

One of the side-effects of the anti-terrorist measures adopted throughout the world in the wake of the attacks on 11 September 2001 was to legitimise reinforced government strategies to contain global social movements, under the pretext that they help promote extreme violence. The chief danger of legislation inspired by such security-minded thinking is that the definition of terrorism, on which there has never been an international consensus, will be extended to cover every form of dissidence.

Encouraged by the high visibility and effectiveness of cyber-mobilisation set off by social actors at the worldwide level, every imaginable persuasion on the political spectrum soon concluded that a 'global civil society' had arrived. The expression even entered the language of diplomacy and military strategy. The manipulation of the notion should give us pause, however, especially since the notion of 'civil society' in itself is weighed down by a long, ambiguous history.

Such an extrapolation deliberately ignores the complexity of the reconfigurations affecting the nation-state in its links to national civil society, given that both are confronted by the logic of globalisation. It reflects a refusal to rethink the mediation of the state outside of the superficial notions about the 'end of the nation-state'. Whether we like it or not, the territory of the nation-state remains the historical and functional framework for the exercise of democracy, the place where the social contract is defined. It is therefore far from having reached the degree of obsolescence suggested by the crusaders promoting an end to territories through networks. It takes the short-sightedness of techno-libertarians to join in with this sort of 'globalitarian' populism which brandishes a simplistic idea of the state as something abstract and evil and opposed to a sovereign civil society. Despite all the discourse relativising the role of the nation-state, state-to-state negotiations are still required to impose a balance of forces capable of curbing the abuses of ultra-*laissez-faire* economies. Indeed, one of the tasks of organised civil society is also to ensure that the state does not dispossess itself of its own regulatory role.

The attraction exercised by the feats of the technical network goes hand in hand with the idea that all earlier forms of social resistance are obsolete, as well as with an erroneous reading of the particular history of contemporary social networks with a planetary reach. Just as the architects of the 'Revolution in Military Affairs' swept the conflicts of the 'agrarian age' or the 'industrial age' from the strategic map of world conflicts, the high-tech focus tends to rule out the way social demands were formulated in the pre-computer age. Yet, in contemporary struggles against the project for a techno-global order, proven modes of resistance are combined with new ones, just as new forms of exploitation and oppression mix with older ones. Peasant movements whose origins and forms of struggle are rooted in a specific place – from landless peasants in Brazil to French peasants protesting against junk food diets ('la malbouffe') – are one expression, among others, of the patient work of reformulating modes of resistance undertaken throughout the world since the end of the 1970s by many grassroots organisations working at the local, national and international levels. Though their interests and demands cannot always be reconciled, the trade unions, associations and other social movements, engaged in struggles they thought were isolated, have now begun to realise that together they form a planetary chain of resistance (Waterman, 2001).

The experiences of some serve as an example influencing others, as was shown, for example, at the First World Social Forum in Porto Alegre, Brazil, in January 2001. The aim of the event, conceived as a reply to the economic forum for global decision-makers in Davos, Switzerland, was to move beyond the stage of grievances and begin formulating alternative proposals to the ultra-neoliberal model of globalisation. This objective was especially important insofar as many movements tend to bypass the necessary phase of theoretical formulation in the name of the priority of action in the field. The counterpart of this proliferation of discussion at Porto Alegre, was that the organisers chose not to formulate final conclusions. The Second World Social Forum, also held in Porto Alegre, in February 2002, testified to the increasing variety of forms of social interaction emanating from the grassroots level, pervading national societies and ultimately achieving true global reach.

No doubt, these fragmented resistance movements and struggles still have a long way to go before they converge strategically and acquire the weight they need to influence collective decisions. This is particularly true for the decisions pertaining to the design of the so-called global information society. Paradoxically, this structural and eminently political issue has still not received the attention it deserves on the agenda for reflection of the majority of grassroots organisations guided by the new 'feeling of humanity'. The expression 'feeling of humanity', it may be recalled, was forged by the revolutionaries of 1789 to signify the ideal that ceaselessly pushes individual societies to seek higher forms of integration in a universal community.

Conclusion

Intelligence and sensibility are undergoing a genuine mutation due to the new computer technology that is increasingly insinuating itself in the inner workings of our human sensibility, gestures and intelligence. We are currently witnessing a mutation of subjectivity that may be even more important than the invention of writing or printing. . . . A renewal of democracy may have as its aim the pluralistic management of all its machine components. (Félix Guattari, 'Founding Social Practices Anew', 1993)

The genealogical approach that inspired the perspective adopted here on the so-called information society is based on both a conviction and a project: no pedagogical effort to foster grassroots appropriation of technology can neglect the critique of words which, though presented as having no national roots, nevertheless continually find their way into ordinary language and frame our collective representations. It is through these words that the meanings of the concepts of freedom and democracy have undergone important shifts and through them, as well, that we are invited to accept, as an obvious necessity, the reality that now exists and the one that is supposedly emerging.

The discourse accompanying the information society has promoted the notion of *tabula rasa* to the status of a principle. There is nothing that cannot be considered obsolete. Techno-mercantile determinism gives rise to an amnesiac modernity, bereft of any social project. Endless and unlimited communication is being established as the heir of endless and unlimited progress. In the absence of memory, we are seeing eschatology come back into favour, with religious connotations drawn from prophecies concerning the advent of the noosphere (Mattelart, 1999; Noble, 1999). The notion of 'complexity' itself has been perverted and turned into an alibi. The increasing complication of contemporary society dissolves into simple explanations. Bestsellers on the promised future society announce that we are entering 'an era of optimism', and any attitude that does not conform to this positivism is immediately labelled 'technophobic' or 'anti-modern'. The old demons of anti-intellectual populism are surfacing. The technocratic project of reconciling the culture of managers with the culture of intellectuals has been dusted off and recycled. In a book entitled *Postcapitalist Society*, Peter Drucker makes this a prerequisite for the success of the global project of a knowledge-based society: 'They [intellectuals and managers] are opposites; but they relate to each other as poles rather than as contradictions. They surely need each other. . . . The intellectual's world, unless counterbalanced by the manager, becomes one in which everybody "does his own thing" but nobody achieves anything' (Drucker, 1990: 215). But the ideal of modernity he promised is a way of dressing up the project to Westernise the world: 'The material civilization (of the future) and its knowledges all rest on Western foundations. . . . Tomorrow's educated person will have to be prepared for life in a global world. It will be a "Westernized" world', concludes Drucker. By having us believe that access via the Internet to 'universal knowledge', necessarily drawing on the monopolies of existing knowledge, can resolve not only the digital divide but also the social divide, the education experts of the large financial institutions such as the World Bank breathe new life into the diffusionist conception of development, which should have been considered obsolete with the failure of strategies inspired by the quantitative ideology of modernisation. Network society is thus far from having overcome the ethnocentrism of the imperial age. Rather than solving this problem, technology has merely displaced it, leaving the troubling practical question of how new models of development can be conceived and implemented.

The so-called contemporary information revolution makes all the residents of the earth candidates for an umpteenth version of modernisation. The world is divided into fast and slow lanes. Speed becomes the authoritative argument laying the foundation for a lawless world in which the *res publica* is abolished. As an expert at the Rand Corporation states, 'Regulation is abhorred. Neither producers nor users in the information-technology market have the time or the patience for regulation' (Gompert, 1998: 25). In the name of speed, the slow, cumulative historical process of building culture is being drastically altered, as it was a century ago in so-called primitive societies when the heralds of infinite progress imposed a forced march towards modernisation.

This careless attitude towards the long view, which is rife in discourse on the 'information age', is matched only by the discourse on the 'global age'. It is as if the movement of unification of the world had appeared only recently. Retrospective analysis, when it takes place, concerns periods of one or two decades at the most. The dictatorship of the short term certifies as genuinely new, and therefore revolutionary, changes that in fact testify to structural developments and processes that have been under way for a very long time.

It is not only a critical approach that is missing, but also quite simply intellectual curiosity. The lack of an adequate pedagogical approach to digital technologies goes hand in hand with a fascination with technological objects and ignorance of the history of utopian pedagogical thought, which appeared long before the new interactive communication and multimedia technologies. Informational neo-Darwinism must be countered by a new conception of technological systems, bringing into play the creative forces in science, the arts and social innovation. This will require reflection on the myriad interconnections among the modes of social, cultural and educational mediation through which the uses of digital technology are formed, and which are the very source of democratic life. It will mean overcoming the neo-Fordist fetish of speed and developing other relationships with time. Only then may it one day be possible to assert, without fear or any danger of lapsing into prophecy, that the upheaval in our ways of knowing implied by the mutation in technology and science indeed calls into question the very notion of historical time itself. 'You can't change the future' claims the title of a poster advertising a light comedy in Paris. It is up to us to refute this witticism by refusing to accept the commonplaces of technoglobal millenarianism.

Bibliography

Translators' note: Where a work is available in English translation, we have quoted from the English text. In such cases, page references refer to the translation rather than the original-language edition.

Anselmo, J. (1995) 'Satellite Data Plays Key Role in Bosnia Peace Treaty', *Aviation Week and Space Technology*, 11 December.

Armstrong, M. (1999) 'Technology and Public Policy. The Global Communication Revolution'. Address delivered as the Public Policy Keynote, Telecom 99, Geneva, 11 October.

Aron, R. (1955) *L'Opium des intellectuels*. Paris: Calmann-Lévy. (In English, *The Opium of the Intellectuals*. New York: Doubleday, 1957.)

Aron, R. (1962) *Dix-huit leçons sur la société industrielle*. Paris: Gallimard. (In English, *18 Lectures on Industrial Society*. London, 1967.)

Arquilla, J. and Ronfeldt, D. (1998) *The Zapatista Social Netwar in Mexico*. Santa Monica, CA: Rand Corp.

Arquilla. J. and Ronfeldt, D. (1999) *The Emergence of Noopolitik: Toward an American Information Strategy*. Santa Monica, CA: Rand Corp.

Attali, J. and Stourdzé, Y. (1977) 'The Slow Death of Monologue in French Society', in I. de Sola Pool (ed.), *The Social Impact of the Telephone*. Cambridge, MA: MIT Press.

Australian Telecommunications Commission (1975) *Telecom 2000: An Exploration of the Long-Term Development*. Melbourne.

Babbage, C. (1832) *On the Economy of Machinery and Manufactures*. London: A.M. Kelley.

Babbage, C. (1851) *The Exposition of 1851*. London: J. Murray.

Bacon, F. (1996) *Francis Bacon. A Critical Edition of the Major Works*, B. Vickers ed. Oxford: Oxford University Press.

Bangemann, M. (1994) *Europe and the Global Information Society*. Brussels: European Commission.

Barlow, J. P. (1996) 'A Declaration of the Independence of Cyberspace' online: http://www.eff.org/pub/publications/John_Perry. Barlow/barlow_0296. declaration.

Barnaby, T. (1986) *The Automated Battlefield*, New York: The Free Press.

Becker, J. (ed.) (1987) *Transborder Data Flow and Development*. Bonn: Friedrich-Ebert Stiftung.

Beer, S. (1972) *The Brain of the Firm*. London: Allen Lane.

Beer, S. (1975) 'Fanfare for Effective Freedom. Cybernetics Praxis in Government', in *Platform for Change*. New York: Wiley.

Bell, D. (1960) *The End of Ideology: On the Exhaustion of Political Ideas in the Fifties*. New York: The Free Press.

Bell, D. (ed.) (1962) *The Radical Right*. New York: Anchor Books.

Bell, D. (1963) 'Les Formes de l'expression culturelle', *Communications* 2.

Bell, D. (ed.) (1968) *Toward the Year 2000*. Boston: Houghton Mifflin.

Bell, D. (1973) *The Coming of Post-Industrial Society. A Venture in Social Forecasting*. New York: Basic Books.

Bell, D. (1976) *The Cultural Contradictions of Capitalism*. New York: Basic Books.

Bell, D. (1979) 'The Social Framework of the Information Society', in M. Dertouzos and J. Moses (eds), *The Computer Age: A Twenty Year View*. Cambridge, MA: MIT Press.

Bell, D. (1999) 'Foreword', in *The Coming of Post-Industrial Society*, 3rd edn. New York: Basic Books.

Bellardo, T. and Buckland, M. (eds) (1998) *Historical Studies in Information Science*. Medford, NJ: Information Today Inc. (ASIS monograph series)

Belloc, H. (1912) *The Servile State*. Indianapolis: Liberty Fund (reprint) 1977.

Bender, G. and Druckrey, T. (eds) (1994) *Culture on the Brink. Ideologies of Technology*. Seattle: Bay Press.

Beninger, J. (1986) *The Control Revolution: Technological and Economic Origins of the Information Society*. Cambridge, MA: Harvard University Press.

Bjorn-Andersen, Earl M., Holst, O. and Mumford, E. (eds) (1982) *Information Society. For Richer, For Poorer*. Amsterdam: North-Holland/Elsevier.

Boaz, D. (2000) 'Entretien', *Le Monde: Cahier d'économie*, 25 January.

Borges, J. L. (1957) *Otras Inquisiciones*. Buenos Aires: Emece.

Braudel, F. (1958) 'Histoire et sciences sociales. La longue durée', *Annales (Economies, Sociétés, Civilisations)*, 13 (4) October–December.

Braudel, F. (1979) *Civilisation matérielle, économie et capitalisme XVe–XVIIIe siècle*. Paris: Armand Colin, vol. 3. (In English, *Civilisation and Capitalism: 15th–18th Centuries*, trans. S. Reynolds. London: Collins, 1984, vol. 3.)

Breton, P. (1987) *Histoire de l'informatique*. Paris: La Découverte.

Breton, P. (2000) *Le Culte d'Internet*. Paris: La Découverte.

Brzezinski, Z. (1970) *Between Two Ages, America's Role in the Technetronic Era*. London: Penguin.

Brzezinski, Z. (1974) 'Recognizing the Crisis', *Foreign Policy*, 17.

Burch, S. (1999) *ALAI: A Latin American Experience in Social Networking: Women@internet*. New York: Zed Books.

Burke, E. (1986) *Reflections on the Revolution in France*. London: Penguin. First published in 1790.

Burnham, J. (1941) *The Managerial Revolution*. Bloomington: Indiana University Press.

Burton, J. W. (1976) 'The Dynamics of Change in World Society', *Journal of International Studies*, 5 (1) Spring.

Bush, V. (1980) *Science, the Endless Frontier*. New York: Arno Press.

Canguilhem, G. (1966) *Le Normal et le pathologique*. Paris: PUF.

Canguilhem, G. (1989) *La Connaissance de la vie*. Paris: Vrin.

Carey, J. (1975) 'A Cultural Approach to Communication', *Communication*, 1 (2).

Carlyle, T. (1843) *Past and Present*. London: Chapman.

Castells, M. (1996) *The Age of Information. (vol. 1) The Rise of Network Society*. Oxford: Blackwell.

Chandler, A. (1977) *The Visible Hand. The Managerial Revolution in American Business*. Cambridge, MA: Harvard University Press.

Chevalier, M. (1837) *Lettres sur l'Amérique du nord*. Paris: Librairie C. Gosselin. (In English, *Society, Manners and Politics in the United States*, Boston: Weeks and Jordan, 1839.)

Chevalier, M. (1852) 'Chemins de fer', in *Dictionnaire de l'économie politique*. Paris.

Christians, C. G. and Real, M. R. (1979) 'Jacques Ellul's Contributions to Critical Media Theory', *Journal of Communication*, 29 (1).

Condorcet, M. J. A. (1794) *Esquisse d'un tableau historique des progrès de l'esprit humain* . Paris: Flammarion, 1988. (In English, *Sketch for a Historical Picture of the Progress of the Human Mind*, trans. J. Barraclough. Westport, CT: Hyperion Press, 1955.)

Cronberg, T. and Sangregorio, I. L. (1981) 'More on the Same: The Impact of Information Technology on Domestic Life in Japan', *Development Dialogue*, 2.

Crozier, M., Huntington, S. and Watanuki, J. (1975) *The Crisis of Democracy. Report on the Governability of Democracies to the Trilateral Commission*. Prefaced by Z. Brzezinski. New York: New York University Press.

Day, R. E. (2001) *The Modern Invention of Information. Discourse, History and Power*. Carbonale and Edwardville: Southern Illinois University Press.

De Cindio, F. and De Michelis, G. (eds) (1980) *Il Progetto Cybersyn: Cibernetica per la democrazia*. Milano: CLUP-CLUED.

Deleuze, G. (1990) *Pourparlers*. Paris: Minuit.

Deleuze, G. and Guattari, F. (1991) *Qu'est-ce que la philosophie?* Paris: Minuit.

Dertouzos, M. (1999) 'Entretien', *Le Monde*, 23 February.

Desrosières, A. (1993) *La Politique des grands nombres*. Paris: La Découverte.

Dickson, D. (1974) *Alternative Technology and the Politics of Technological Change*. London: Fontana.

Dickson, P. (1971) *Think Tanks*. New York: Ballantine Books.

Downing, J. (2000) *Radical Media, Rebellious Communication and Social Movement*. London: Sage.

Drucker, P. (1969) *The Age of Discontinuity. Guidelines to our Changing Society*. New York: Harper and Row.

Drucker, P. (1990) *Post-capitalist Society*. New York: Harper Business.

Dubos, R. (1970) *Reason Awake: Science for Man*. New York: Columbia University Press.

Dyson, E., Gilder, G., Keyworth, G. and Toffler, A. (1994) 'The Cyberspace and the American Dream: A Magna Carta for the Knowledge Age', release 1. 2. Progress for Freedom Foundation, 22 August.

Edwards, P. N. (1989) 'The Closed World: Systems Discourse, Military Policy, and Post-World War II US Historical Consciousness', in L. Levidow and K. Robins (eds), *The Military Information Society*. London: Free Association Books.

Ellul, J. (1954) *La Technique ou l'enjeu du siècle*. Paris: A. Colin. (In English, *The Technological Society*. trans. J. Wilkinson. intro. R. K. Merton. New York: Vintage, 1964.)

Ellul, J. (1962) *Propagandes*. Paris: A. Colin. (In English, *Propaganda. The Formation of Men's Attitudes*, trans. K. Kellen and J. Lerner. New York: Knopf, 1965.)

Emerson, R. W. (1883) 'Historic Notes of Life and Letters in New England' (1865), in *Emerson's Works*, ed. J. E. Cabot. Boston and New York: Houghton, Mifflin.

Etzioni, A. (1968) *The Active Society, A Theory of Societal and Political Processes*. New York: The Free Press.

Etzioni, A. (1995) *The Spirit of Community. Rights, Responsibilities and the Communitarian Agenda*. London: Fontana.

Etzioni, A. and Leonard, E. (1971) 'Minerva: A Participatory Technology System', *Bulletin of Atomic Scientists*, November.

Eurobit/ITI/Jeida (1995) *Global Information Infrastructure*. Tripartite Preparatory Meeting, 26–27 January.

European Commission (April, 1997) *Building the European Information Society for Us All. Final Report*. Brussels: Directorate General V.

Ewald, F. (1986) *L'Etat Providence*. Paris: Grasset.

Fitoussi, J. P. et al. (2000) *Rapport sur l'état de l'Union européenne*. Paris: Fayard-Presses de Sciences Po.

Flichy, P. (1991) *Une Histoire de la communication moderne*. Paris: La Découverte. (In English, *Dynamics of Modern Communication: The Shaping and Impact of New Communication Technology*, trans. L. Libbrecht. London: Sage, 1995.)

Flichy, P. (1999) 'Internet ou la communauté scientifique idéale', *Réseaux*, 97.

Foucault, M. (1993) *Les Mots et les choses*. Paris: Gallimard. (In English, *The Order of Things. An Archeology of Human Sciences*, trans. A. Sheridan. London: Tavistock Publications, 1970; Routledge, 1993.)

Foucault, M. (1975) *Surveiller et punir*. Paris: Gallimard. (In English, *Discipline and Punish: The Birth of the Prison*, trans. A. Sheridan. London: Penguin, 1977.)

Fourier, C. (1969) *Le Nouveau Monde amoureux*. Paris: Anthropos. (In English, excerpts in *The Utopian Vision of Charles Fourier: Selected Texts on Work, Love, and Passionate Attraction*, trans. and ed. J. Beecher and R. Bienvenu. Boston: Beacon Press, 1971.)

Friedmann, G. (1949) 'Les Technocrates et la civilisation technicienne', in G. Gurvitch (ed.), *Industrialisation et technocratie*. Paris: A. Colin.

Fuwei, S. (1996) *Cultural Flow between China and Outside World throughout History*. Beijing: Foreign Languages Press.

Garnham, N. (1990) *Capitalism and Global Communication: Global Culture and the Politics of Information*. London: Sage.

Garnham, N. (2000) 'La Théorie de la société de l'information en tant qu'idéologie', *Réseaux*, 18 (101).

Gates, B. (1995) *The Road Ahead*. New York: Viking Penguin.

Gerbner, G., Gross, L. and Melody, W. H. (eds) (1973) *Communications Technology and Social Policy*. New York: Wiley.

Giddens, A. (1999) *The Third Way. The Renewal of Social Democracy*. Cambridge: Polity Press.

Giraud, A., Missika, J. L. and Wolton, D. (1978) *Les Réseaux pensants. Télécommunications et société*. Paris: Masson.

Gompert, D. C. (1998) 'Right Makes Might: Freedom and Power in the Information Age', *Headline Series, Foreign Policy Association*, 316 (Fall).

Goody, J. (1977) *The Domestication of the Savage Mind*. Cambridge: Cambridge University Press.

Gore, A. (1994) *Remarks Prepared for Delivery by Vice-President Al Gore to the International Telecommunications Union (Buenos Aires, March 21)*. Washington: Department of State.

Gramsci, A. (1971) *Selections from the Prison Notebooks*, eds Q. Hoare and G. Nowell Smith. London: Lawrence and Wishart. First published in Italian in 1929.

Guattari, F. (1993) 'Refonder les pratiques sociales', *Manière de voir/Le Monde diplomatique*, 19 (September).

Guerlac, H. (1986) 'Vauban: The Impact of Science on War', in P. Paret (ed.), *Makers of Modern Strategy*. Princeton, NJ: Princeton University Press.

Guillaume, M. (ed.) (1999) *Où vont les autoroutes de l'information?* Paris: Descartes.

Gumucio Dagron, A. (2001) *Making Waves. Stories of Participatory Communication for Social Change. A Report to the Rockefeller Foundation*. New York: The Rockefeller Foundation.

Halévy, D. (1923) *Vauban*. Paris: Grasset.

Hamelink, C. (2000) *The Ethics of Cyberspace*. London: Sage.

Huntington, S. (1968) 'Political Development and the Decline of the American System of World Order', in D. Bell (ed.), *Toward the Year 2000*. Boston: Houghton Mifflin.

Huntington, S. (1999) 'The Lonely Superpower'. *Foreign Affairs*, 78 (2).

Huxley, A. (1932) *Brave New World*. London: Harper Collins.

Illich, I. (1973) *Tools for Conviviality*. New York: Harper and Row.

Innis, H. (1950) *Empire and Communications*. Toronto: University of Toronto Press.

Innis, H. (1951) *The Bias of Communication*. Toronto: University of Toronto Press.

International Telecommunications Union (1998) *World Telecommunication Development Report*. Geneva: ITU.

Jacob, F. (1970) *La Logique du vivant*. Paris: Gallimard. (In English, *The Logic of Life: A History of Heredity*, trans. B. E. Spillmann. New York: Vintage, 1973.)

Jacobson, J. (1979) *Technical Change. Employment and Technological Dependency*. Lund (Sweden): Research Policy Institute, University of Lund.

Jacudi (Japan Computer Usage Development Institute) (1971) *Plan for an Information Society. A National Goal for the Year 2000*. Tokyo.

Jakobson, R. (1962) *Selected Writings*. The Hague: Mouton.

Jennings, H. (1987) *Pandaemonium. The Coming of the Machine Seen by Contemporary Observers*, M. L. Jennings and C. Madge eds. London: Picador.

Jouët, J. (1987) *L'Écran apprivoisé: télématique et informatique à domicile*. Paris: Cnet.

Jouët, J. (2000) 'Retour critique sur la sociologie des usages', *Réseaux*, 100.

Joxe, A (1996) *Le Débat stratégique américain 1995–96. Révolution dans les affaires militaires*. Paris: Cirpes.

Julia, D. (1981) *Les trois couleurs du tableau noir. La Révolution*. Paris: Bélin.

Kahn, H. and Wiener, A. (1967) *The Year 2000: A Framework for Speculation on the Next Thirty-Three Years*, intro. by D. Bell. New York: Macmillan.

Kapor, M. (1993) 'Where Is the Digital Highway Really Heading? The Case for a Jeffersonian Information Policy', *Wired*, 1 (3).

Keohane, R. O. and Nye J. S. (eds) (1972) *Transnational Relations and World Politics*. Cambridge, MA: Harvard University Press.

Keohane, R. O. and Nye J. S. (1998) 'Power and Interdependence in the Information Age', *Foreign Affairs*, 77 (5).

Kerkhove, D. (de) (1990) 'La Foi en l'Eglise de Marshall McLuhan', *Communication et Langages*, 85.

Klare, M. T. (1972) *War without End*. New York: Vintage.

Krantz, M. (1996) 'Cashing in on Tomorrow', *Time*, 15 July.

Kroloff, G. and Cohen, S. (1977) *The New Information Order. Report to the US Senate*. Washington, DC: Committee on Foreign Relations.

Kropotkin, P. (1912) *Fields, Factories and Workshops*. London: Thomas Nelson. First published in 1899.

Kula, W. (1984) *Les Mesures et les hommes*. Paris: Editions de la Maison des sciences de l'homme. (In English, *Measures and Men*. Princeton, NJ: Princeton University Press, 1986.)

La Mettrie, J. O. (de) (1981) *L'Homme-machine*. Paris: Denoël.

Lacroix, J. G. and Tremblay, G. (1997) 'The "Information Society" and Cultural Industries Theory', *Current Sociology*, 45 (4) October.

La Fontaine, H. and Otlet, P. (1912) 'La Vie internationale et l'effort pour son organisation', *La Vie internationale*, 1 (1).

Landes, D. S. (1983) *Revolution in Time: Clocks and the Making of the Modern World*. Cambridge, MA: Belknap.

Lanteri-Laura, G. (1970) *Histoire de la phrénologie*. Paris: Presses universitaires de France.

Lasswell, H. (1927) *Propaganda Technique in the World War*. NewYork: Knopf.

Lazarsfeld, P. (1970) *Philosophie des sciences sociales*. Paris: Gallimard.

Lefebvre, H. (1967) *Vers le Cybernanthrope*. Paris: Denoël/Gonthier.

Legendre, P. (1997) *La Fabrique de l'homme occidental*. Paris: Arte éditions.

Leroi-Gourhan, A. (1964) *Le Geste et la parole. I. Technique et langage. II. La mémoire et les rythmes*. Paris: Albin Michel.

Lévy, P. (1997) *Cyberculture*. Paris: Odile Jacob.

Lévy, P. (2000) *World Philosophie*. Paris: Odile Jacob.

Lievrouw, L. A. and Livingstone, S. M. (eds) (2001) *The Handbook of New Media: Social Shaping and Consequences of Information and Communication Technologies*. London: Sage.

Lippmann, W. (1922) *Public Opinion*. London: Allen and Unwin.

Lipset, M. S. (1960) *Political Man. The Social Bases of Politics*. New York: Doubleday.

Lyotard, J. F. (1979) *La Condition postmoderne*. Paris: Minuit. (In English, *The Postmodern Condition: A Report on Knowledge*, trans. G. Bennington and B. Massumi. Minneapolis: University of Minnesota Press, 1984.)

Macherey, P. (1992) 'L'Idéologie avant l'idéologie: l'Ecole normale en l'an III', in F. Azouvi (ed.), *L'Institution de la raison*. Paris: Vrin/EHESS.

Machlup, F. (1962) *The Production and Distribution of Knowledge in the United States*. Princeton, NJ: Princeton University Press.

MacIsaac, D. (1986) 'Voices from the Central Blue: The Air Power Theorists', in P. Paret (ed.), *Makers of Modern Strategy*. Princeton, NJ: Princeton University Press.

MacKay, D. M. (1969) *Information, Mechanism and Meaning*. Cambridge, MA: MIT Press.

Madec, A. (1980) *Les Flux transfrontières de données*. Paris: La Documentation française.

Mansell, R. and Silverstone, R. (eds) (1996) *Communication by Design: The Politics of Information and Communication Technologies*. Oxford: Oxford University Press.

Mansell, R. and Wehn, U. (1998) *Knowledge Societies: Information Technology for Sustainable Development*. Oxford: Oxford University Press.

Marshall, A. (1919) *Industry and Trade*. London: Macmillan.

Martin, J. (1978) *The Wired Society*. Englewood Cliffs, NJ: Prentice-Hall.

Masuda, J. (1980) *The Information Society as Post-Industrial Society*. Tokyo: Institute for the Information Society. (US edition, Washington, DC: World Future Society, 1981.)

Mattelart, A. (1976) *Multinationales et systèmes de communication*. Paris: Anthropos. (In English, *Multinational Corporations and the Control of Culture*, trans. M. Chanan. Brighton: Harvester, and Atlantic Highlands, NJ: Humanities Press, 1979.)

Mattelart, A. (1992) *La Communication-monde*. Paris: La Découverte. (In English, *Mapping World Communication. War, Progress, Culture*, trans. S. Emanuel and J. A. Cohen. Minneapolis: University of Minnesota Press, 1994.)

Mattelart, A. (1994) *L'Invention de la communication*. Paris: La Découverte. (In English, *The Invention of Communication*, trans. S. Emanuel. Minneapolis, University of Minnesota Press, 1996.)

Mattelart, A. (1996) *La Mondialisation de la communication*. Paris: Presses universitaires de France. (In English, *Networking the World (1794–2000)*, trans. L. Carey-Libbrecht and J. A. Cohen. Minneapolis: University of Minnesota Press, 2000.)

Mattelart, A. (1999) *Histoire de l'utopie planétaire. De la cité prophétique à la société globale*. Paris: La Découverte.

Mattelart, A. and M. (1995) *Histoire des théories de la communication*. Paris, La Découverte. (In English, *Theories of Communication. A Short Introduction*, trans. S. Gruenheck Taponier and J. A. Cohen. London: Sage, 1998.)

Mattelart, A. and Schmucler, H. (1983) *L'Ordinateur et le tiers monde*. Paris: Maspero. (In English, *Communication and Information Technologies. Freedom of Choice for Latin America ?*, trans. D. Buxton. Norwood, NJ: Ablex, 1985.)

Mattelart, A. and Stourdzé, Y. (1982) *Technologie, Culture et Communication. Rapport au Ministre de la recherche et de l'industrie*. Paris: La Documentation française. (In English, *Technology, Culture and Communication. A Report to the French Minister of Research and Industry*, trans. D. Buxton. Amsterdam: North Holland-Elsevier, 1985.)

Mattelart, T. (1995) *Le Cheval de Troie audiovisuel. Le rideau de fer à l'épreuve des radios et télévisions transfrontières*. Grenoble: PUG.

McBride, S. (ed.) (1980) *Many Voices, One World*. Paris: Unesco.

McChesney, R. W. (1997) *Corporate Media and the Threat to Democracy*. New York: Seven Stories Press.

McChesney, R. W., Bellamy Foster, J., Meiskins-Wood, F. (eds) (1998) *Capitalism and the Information Age*. New York: Monthly Review Press.

McLuhan, M. (1962) *The Gutenberg Galaxy*. Toronto: Toronto University Press.

McLuhan, M. (1964) *Understanding Media*. London: Ark Paperbacks.

McLuhan, M. and Fiore, Q. (1968) *War and Peace in the Global Village*. New York: Bantam.

Meadows, D. H. et al. (1972) *The Limits to Growth: A Report of the Club of Rome's Project on the Predicament of Mankind*. New York: Universe Books.

Meier, R. (1962) *A Communications Theory of Urban Growth*. Cambridge, MA: Joint Center for Urban Studies of MIT and Harvard University, MIT Press.

Miège, B. (1997) *La Société conquise par la communication* (vol. 1) and *La Communication entre l'industrie et l'espace public* (vol. 2) Grenoble: PUG.

Miège, B. (2000) *Les industries du contenu face à l'ordre informationnel.* Grenoble: PUG.

Moeglin, P. (ed.) (1998) *L'Industrialisation de la formation. Etat de la question.* Paris: Centre national de documentation pédagogique.

Morin, E. (1974) 'La nature de la société', *Communications,* 22.

Mosco. V. (1989) *The Pay-per Society: Computers and Communication in the Information Age.* Toronto: Garamond Press.

Mosco, V. (1996) *The Political Economy of Communication, Rethinking and Renewal.* London: Sage.

Mumford, L. (1934) *Technics and Civilization.* New York: Harcourt, Brace and World.

Mumford, L. (1967) *The Myth of the Machine. Technics and Human Development.* New York: Harcourt Brace Jovanovich.

Mumford, L. (1970) *The Myth of the Machine. The Pentagon of Power.* New York: Harcourt Brace Jovanovich.

Muskat, M. (ed.) (1973) *The Changing International Community.* The Hague: Mouton.

Musso, P. (1997) *Télécommunications et philosophie des réseaux.* Paris: Presses universitaires de France.

National Aeronautics and Space Administration (NASA) (1971) *Communication for Social Needs, Technological Opportunities. A Study for the President's Domestic Council.* Final Report, 24 September.

Negroponte, N. (1995) *Being Digital.* New York: Vintage.

Neveu, E. (1994) *Une Société de communication?* Paris: Montchrestien.

Noble, D. F. (1999) *The Religion of Technology: The Divinity of Man and the Spirit of Invention.* London: Penguin.

Nora, P. and Minc, A. (1978) *L'Informatisation de la société.* Paris: La Documentation française. (In English, *The Computerization of Society*, intro. by D. Bell. Cambridge, MA: MIT Press, 1980.)

Nordenstreng, K. and Schiller, H. (eds) (1993) *Beyond National Sovereignty International Communication in the 1990s.* Norwood, NJ: Ablex.

Nye, J. S. (1990) *Bound to Lead: The Changing Nature of American Power.* New York: Basic Books.

Nye, J. S. and Owens, W. A. (1996) 'America's Information Edge'. *Foreign Affairs,* 75 (2).

OECD (1979) *Interfutures. Facing the Future: Mastering the Probable and Managing the Unpredictable.* Paris: OECD.

Oettinger, A. G. (1980) 'Information Resources: Knowledge and Power in the 21st Century', *Science,* 209.

Ohmae, K. (1985) *The Triad Power.* New York: The Free Press.

Ohmae, K. (1995) *The End of the Nation State: The Rise of Regional Economies.* London: HarperCollins.

Otlet, P. (1919) *La Société intellectuelle des Nations*. Paris: Alcan.

Otlet, P. (1934) *Traité de documentation, le livre sur le livre*. Brussels: Mundaneum.

Owens, W. (2001) *Lifting the Fog of War*. Baltimore: Johns Hopkins University Press.

Paine, T. (1791) *Rights of Man*. Ware, Hertfordshire: Wordsworth, 1996.

Palmer, M. and Tunstall, J. (1990) *Liberating Communication. Policy-Making in France and Britain*. London: Blackwell.

Parent, M. (1982) *Vauban, un Encyclopédiste avant la lettre*. Paris: Berger-Levrault.

Penty, A. J. (1917) *Old World for New: A Study of the Post-Industrial State*. London: Allen and Unwin.

Penty, A. J. (1922) *Post-Industrialism*. London: Allen and Unwin.

Porat, M. U. (1977) *The Information Economy: Definition and Measurement*. Washington, DC: Government Printing Office.

Porat, M. U. (1978) 'Global Implications of the Information Society', *Journal of Communication*, 28 (1).

Pratt, V. (1987) *The Evolution of Artificial Intelligence*. Oxford: Basil Blackwell.

Progress and Freedom Foundation (May, 1995) *The Telecom Revolution: An American Opportunity*. Washington, DC.

Proulx, S. and Vitalis, A. (eds) (1999) *Vers une citoyenneté simulée. Médias, réseaux et mondialisation*. Rennes: Apogée.

Quéau, P. (1993) *Virtuels. Vertus et vertiges*. Paris: Champ Vallon-INA.

Quételet, A. (1835) *Sur l'homme et le développement de ses facultés ou essai de physique sociale*. Paris: Bachelier.

Raboy, M. (1990) *Missed Opportunities: The Story of Canada's Broadcasting Policy*. Montreal and Toronto: McGill & Queen's University Press.

Raboy, M. (ed.) (2001) *Global Media Policy in the New Millenium*. Lutton: Lutton University Press.

Rada, J. (1981) *The Impact of Microelectronics: A Tentative Appraisal of Information Technology*. Geneva: BIT/ILO.

Ramonet, I., Cassen, B. and Gresh, A. (eds) (1996) *Internet L'extase et l'effroi*. Paris: Manière de voir/*Le Monde diplomatique*.

Ramonet, I., Cassen, B. and Halimi, S. (eds) (1999) *Révolution dans la communication*. Paris: Manière de voir/*Le Monde diplomatique*.

Reich, R. (1991) *The Work of Nations. Preparing Ourselves for 21st Century Capitalism*. New York: Knopf.

Reich, R. (1997) 'Entretien: Il faut parier sur la formation', *Sciences Humaines* (hors série), 17 (June–July).

Rheingold, H. (1993) *The Virtual Community*. Reading, MA: Addison-Wesley.

Richta, R. (1969) *La Civilisation au carrefour*. Paris: Anthropos.

Richta, R., Klein, O., Levcik, B. and Dubska, I. (1969) 'The Perspective of the Scientific and Technological Revolution'. in R. Jungk and J. Galtung (eds), *Mankind 2000*. London: Allen and Unwin.

Riesman, D. et al. (1950) *The Lonely Crowd: A Study of the Changing American Character*. New Haven: Yale University Press.

Robins, K. and Webster, F. (1999) *Times of Technoculture. From the Information Society to the Virtual Life*. London: Routledge.

Rodotà, S. (1999) *La Démocratie électronique*. Rennes: Apogée.

Rostow, W. W. (1960) *The Stages of Economic Growth: A Non-Communist Manifesto*. Cambridge: Cambridge University Press.

Roszak, T. (1972) *Where the Wasteland Ends: Politics and Transcendence in Post-industrial Society*. New York: Doubleday.

Roszak, T. (1994) *The Cult of Information*. Berkeley: University of California Press.

Rougemont, D. (de) (1981) 'Information n'est pas savoir', *Diogène*, 116.

Saint-Simon, C. H. (de) (1821) *Du Système industriel*. Paris: Renouard.

Sassen, S. (1994) *Cities in a World Economy*. Thousand Oaks, CA: Sage.

Schiller, H. (1976) *Communication and Cultural Domination*. White Plains, NY: Sharpe.

Schiller, H. (1984) *Information and the Crisis Economy*. Norwood, NJ: Ablex.

Schiller, H. (2000) *Living in the Number One Country*. New York: Seven Stories Press.

Schiller, D. (2000) *Digital Capitalism. Networking the Global Market System*. Cambridge, MA: MIT Press.

Schlesinger, P. (1997) 'From Cultural Defence to Political Culture', *Media, Culture & Society*, 19.

Schmucler, H. (1997) *Memoria de la comunicación*. Buenos Aires: Biblos.

Schumacher, E. F. (1973) *Small is beautiful: Economics as if People Mattered*. New York: Harper and Row.

Sénécal, M. (1995) *L'Espace médiatique*. Montréal: Liber.

Serres, M. (1968) *Le système de Leibniz et ses modèles mathématiques*. Paris: Presses universitaires de France.

Sfez, L. (1988) *Critique de la communication*. Paris: Seuil.

Shannon, C. and Weaver, W. (1949) *The Mathematical Theory of Communication*. Urbana-Champaign, IL: University of Illinois Press.

Shils, E. (1955) 'The End of Ideology?' *Encounter*, 5 (5).

Shils, E. (1960) 'Mass Society and Its Culture', *Daedalus*, Spring.

Singhal, A. and Rogers, E. (2001) *India's Communication Revolution: From Bullock Carts to Cyber Marts*. New Delhi: Sage.

Slack, J. and Fejes, F. (eds) (1987) *The Ideology of the Information Age*. Norwood, NJ: Ablex.

Smith, A. (1930) *An Inquiry into the Nature and Causes of the Wealth of Nations*, E. Cannan (ed.). London: Methuen. First published in 1776.

Smithson, S. (2001) 'Entretien', *Le Monde*, 9 January.

Smythe, D. (1980) *Dependency Road: Communications, Capitalism, Consciousness*. Norwood, NJ: Ablex.

Sola Pool, I. (de) (1974) 'The Rise of Communications Policy Research', *Journal of Communication*, 24 (2).

Stiegler, B. (1991) 'Machines à lire', *Autrement*, 121.

Stiegler, B. (1994/1996) *La Technique et le temps*, 2 vols. Paris: Galilée.

Stourdzé, Y. (1987) *Pour une poignée d'électrons. Pouvoir et communication.* Paris: Fayard.

Swett, C. (1995) *Strategic Assessment: The Internet.* Washington, DC: Department of Defense.

Tafuri, M. (1979) *Projet et utopie. Espace et architecture.* Paris: Dunod.

Tarde, G. (1890) *Les Lois de l'imitation. Etude sociologique.* Paris: Alcan.

Taylor, F. W. (1911) *Principles of Scientific Management.* NewYork: Harper.

Teilhard de Chardin, P. (1959) *The Phenomenon of Man.* New York: Harper.

Telecommission Directing Committee (1971) *Instant World: A Report on Telecommunications in Canada.* Ottawa.

Thayer, L. (ed.) (1970) *Communication: General Semantics Perpectives.* New York: Spartan.

Thom, R. (1974) 'Un protée de la sémantique: l'information', in *Modèles mathématiques de la morphogenèse.* Paris: Editions 10/18.

Thomas, T. L. (1999) 'Preventing Conflict Through Information Technology', *Military Review*, December–February.

Thompson, J. and Padover, S. (1963) *Secret Diplomacy: Espionage and Cryptography 1500–1815.* New York: Frederick Ungar. First published in 1937.

Toffler, A. (1970) *Future Shock*, NewYork: Random House.

Toffler, A. (1976) 'La démocratie prospective', *Futuribles*, 7.

Toffler, A. (1980) *The Third Wave.* New York: William Morrow.

Toffler, A. and H. (1993) *War and Anti-War.* New York: Little, Brown.

Touraine, A. (1969) *La Société post-industrielle: naissance d'une société.* Paris: Denoël.

UNDP (1999) *World Report on Human Development.* Geneva: United Nations Development Program.

UNESCO (2001) *Draft Recommandation on the Promotion and Use of Multilingualism and Universal Access to Cyberspace.* Paris: UNESCO.

United Nations Center on Transnational Corporations (1982) *Transnational Corporations and Transborder Data Flows: A Technical Paper.* New York: UN.

United States Senate (1976) *Foreign and Military Intelligence. Book I, Final Report of the Select Committee to Study Governmental Operations, April 26 (Legislative Day, April 14).* Washington: US Government Printing Office.

Vedel, T. (1996) 'Les politiques des autoroutes de l'information dans les pays industrialisés. Une analyse comparative', *Réseaux*, 78.

Virilio, P. (1996) *Cybermonde. La politique du pire.* Paris: Textuel.

Vitalis, A. (1981) *Informatique, pouvoir et libertés.* Paris: Economica.

Vitalis, A. (1998) 'Techniques d'information et formes politiques. La démocratie à l'ère des nouvelles technologies'. *Revue européenne des sciences sociales*, 111.

Wallerstein, I. (1983) *Historical Capitalism.* London: Verso.

Waterman, P. (2001) *Globalization, Social Movements and the New Internationalism.* London: Continuum.

Webster, F. (1995) *Theories of the Information Society.* London: Routledge.

Webster, F. and Robins, K. (1987) *Information Technology: A Luddite Analysis.* Norwood, NJ: Ablex.

Weissberg, J. L. (1999) *Présences à distance. Déplacement virtuel et réseaux numéri-ques*. Paris: L'Harmattan.

Wiener, N. (1948) *Cybernetics or Control and Communication in the Animal and the Machine*. Paris: Hermann.

Wilden, A. (1987) *The Rules Are No Game: The Strategy of Communication*. London: Routledge and Kegan Paul.

Williams, R. (1983) *Keywords: A Vocabulary of Culture and Society*. London: Fontana (revised and expanded edition). First published in 1976.

Wolton, D. (1999) *Internet, et après?* Paris: Flammarion.

World Bank (1998) *The World Development Report 1998/1999. Knowledge for Development*. New York: Oxford University Press.

Zamyatin, Y. (1972) *We*, trans. Mina Ginsburg. New York: Viking Press. First published in 1921.

Zamyatin, Y. (1984) *Islanders and the Fisher of Men*, trans. S. Fuller and J. Saachi. Edinburgh: Salamander Press. First published in 1918.

Index